KENNETH IMO

How History, Sports, and Education Can Inform Diversity, Inclusion, and Equity Today

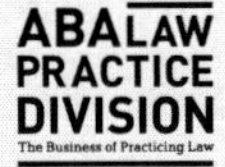

Cover design by Tahiti Spears / ABA Design

Printed in the United States of America.

22 21 20 19 18   5 4 3 2 1

Library of Congress Cataloging-in-Publication Data

Names: Imo, Kenneth, author. | American Bar Association. Law Practice Division, sponsoring body.
Title: Fix it : how history, sports, and education can inform diversity, inclusion and equity today / by Kenneth Imo.
Description: First edition. | Chicago : American Bar Association, 2018. | Includes bibliographical references and index.
Identifiers: LCCN 2018038005 (print) | LCCN 2018038051 (ebook) | ISBN 9781641053044 (ebook) | ISBN 9781641053037 (print : alk. paper)
Subjects: LCSH: Lawyers—United States—Social conditions. | Practice of law—Social aspects—United States. | Diversity in the workplace—United States. | Affirmative action programs—United States.
Classification: LCC KF297 (ebook) | LCC KF297 .I468 2018 (print) | DDC 340.023/73—dc23
LC record available at https://lccn.loc.gov/2018038005

Discounts are available for books ordered in bulk. Special consideration is given to state bars, CLE programs, and other bar-related organizations. Inquire at Book Publishing, ABA Publishing, American Bar Association, 321 N. Clark Street, Chicago, Illinois 60654-7598.

www.ShopABA.org

To Zylius and Gloria Imo:

You came here from Nigeria with $200, two small children and hope. Against the odds, you built a life for yourselves, my siblings and me. I thank you, I admire you, I love you. Kenneth

Contents

About the Author

Prior to joining Capital One's diversity and inclusion leadership team, Kenneth Imo led diversity for two international law firms and was in private practice for approximately a decade. Kenneth began his legal career in the United States Air Force Judge Advocate General Corps as a captain.

Kenneth received his law degree from Wake Forest University School of Law. He attended Southern Methodist University on a football scholarship where he received bachelor's degrees in economics and history.

Kenneth lives in Alexandria, Virginia, with his wife Jennifer, daughters Olivia, Cecilia, and Juliet, and dog Julio Jones.

Letter to the Reader

Dear Reader:

I am a son of immigrants. I am a brother. I am a husband. I am a father. I am a veteran. I am black. I am an American. I'm sure we have a lot in common while having many differences. We may find comfort in commonality, but dissimilarity makes life interesting because it forces us to learn and evolve how we think and problem solve. There is power in difference, but human frailty in the face of the unknown can evoke emotions of fear and resentment resulting in conflict, unfairness, and injustice. Our nation is a collection of differences, and our history includes many examples of the promise and possibilities of a diverse society as well as, unfortunately, the ugliness that accompanies the resistance to change and the lengths people take to preserve a system that benefits them exclusively. This struggle between the dueling perceptions of multiculturalism as a strength or as an ominous development to be feared and contained, by any means, is as old as the republic. We have seen this play out through the abolitionist movement, the Civil War, Reconstruction, Jim Crow, the civil rights movement, and now diversity and inclusion (D&I). Lawyers figured prominently on all sides of the issues in each era.

In 1787, the Constitutional Convention declared an African American as three-fifths of a white person. This became law and lawyers maintained its constitutionality. Most importantly, it created and ingrained a racial caste system. Almost 90 years later, in 1865, the 13th Amendment abolished slavery and the 14th Amendment granted citizenship to formerly enslaved people. These amendments were the law and lawyers upheld them, but resistance to the enfranchisement of black folks was strong. In 1896, the U.S. Supreme Court ushered in the Jim Crow era when it made "separate but equal" constitutional through the *Plessy v. Ferguson*[1] decision. Almost 60 years later, in

1. Plessy v. Ferguson, 163 U.S. 537 (1896).

1954, lawyers successfully fought to make "separate but equal" unconstitutional in *Brown v. Board of Education*.[2] And, in 1967, exactly ten years before I was born, lawyers successfully confronted the illegality of marriages like mine when the Supreme Court ruled unconstitutional the laws banning interracial marriage in *Loving v. Virginia*.[3] But legal decisions alone do not change mindsets, and the struggle for equity continued through the 1960s and into the present day, and the pursuit of D&I is another means by which to address it.

The legal profession, which has been at the heart of the equity movement, has a diversity problem. Despite its best efforts to have a more diverse bar, it just isn't happening. Some of the blame falls on the profession, while some is attributable to factors beyond the profession's control. This book is about both, and it draws on historical and current references and the latest research to tell a story that, I hope, compels action by all of us.

I take a broad approach to the issue of diversity in the legal profession by viewing the profession's diversity pipeline as a funnel with the nation's most diverse population—preschool-aged children—at the top, and one of the nation's least diverse populations—lawyers—eventually pouring out of the very narrow bottom end of the funnel. This book addresses punctures and choke points in the pipeline resulting from institutional unfairness, tradition, and bias that either force out or stall diversity in early education, college, law school, the law firm recruiting process, and, ultimately, in how law firms evaluate and promote lawyers. These factors are barriers. The legal profession may lack the power to address some, but others are self-imposed. Either way, we must be honest about them, so we can confront these barriers effectively and appropriately. And we can look to examples in our nation's history for guidance because these issues aren't new.

The first two chapters recount stories of Harriet Tubman's exploits during the Civil War and the path taken by Branch Rickey to integrate baseball when Jackie Robinson became the first African American to play in Major League Baseball (MLB). Chapter 1 illustrates why D&I is important. This illustration goes beyond diversity as the right thing to do, which it is, and also addresses how it benefits everyone when people who are often overlooked, because they

2. Brown v. Bd. of Educ., 347 U.S. 483 (1954).
3. Loving v. Virginia, 388 U.S. 1 (1967).

may not appear to look the part of a leader, receive opportunities to contribute in ways that benefit their organizations—in Tubman's case, the Union Army.

Chapter 1 also touches upon the consequences of homophily, the attraction people have to folks like themselves. Comfort lies here, but so does discrimination—intended or unintended. This chapter explores the economic and reputational consequences when legislators, business executives, and institutions and their leaders fail to appreciate the importance and impact of D&I. It details the economic consequences of the passage of legislation by the North Carolina General Assembly discriminating against the lesbian, gay, bisexual, transgender, and queer (LGBTQ+) community; the reputational damage to the University of Missouri for failing to adequately address the concerns of students victimized by racist behavior from other students; and the reactions of business leaders to President Donald Trump's inability to unequivocally condemn white supremacists after the events in Charlottesville, Virginia, that resulted in the death of a protester in the summer of 2017.

Chapter 2, on the integration of the MLB, explores the importance of leadership. This chapter answers the question of how leaders promote change. Jackie Robinson was an extraordinary American—a multisport athlete at the University of California, Los Angeles, an Army veteran, a great baseball player who was inducted into the Hall of Fame, and an even better person. In the 1940s, his skin color discounted his pedigree and baseball prowess, to the extent that only one baseball executive had the courage to give Robinson an opportunity to compete at baseball's highest level: Branch Rickey. Rickey knew the rules governing his world, so he understood that he could not just plug Robinson into the MLB. He had to be a student of race, racism, and the obstacles that could potentially impede Robinson's ability to fully showcase his talents. This chapter exemplifies the behavior of a leader wanting to have a real impact. Platitudes and empty proclamations are not enough. D&I progresses when leaders are secure enough to admit their ignorance on a topic and wise enough to become a student of the issue they want to solve. Rickey led with curiosity, empathy, humility, and a willingness to wield his power to effect change.

Chapters 3 through 6 address the barriers to creating a more diverse and inclusive legal profession. Some barriers are institutional, as Chapters 3 and 4 illustrate. Others are artificial due to an unyielding devotion to tradition, which you will see illustrated in Chapters 5 and 6. And other barriers are attributable to environmental and cultural factors influencing our perceptions of ability and how people are positioned for success in various contexts. The first hurdles are erected long before people sit for the Law School Admissions Test (LSAT). In fact, initial obstacles occur before people are born. Because education should be the great equalizer, I devoted Chapters 3 and 4 to looking at it. Chapter 3 addresses the origins of public education, the socioeconomic and racial inequities accompanying its inception, and the use of the legal system to solidify a racial caste system motivated partly by the undereducation of people of color. Chapter 4 discusses the role lawyers played in overturning laws perpetuating unfairness in education and how generations of institutionalized inequity currently impact the readiness of youngsters to become future lawyers.

This unfairness weeds out many students of color well in advance of their submission of applications to college and law school admissions offices. But for the students who make it far enough to be considered for entry into higher education, they must contend with artificial barriers created by these institutions. Colleges and law schools, like society in general, inherited the consequences of this legacy of unfairness, but they are not required to preserve it through self-imposed barriers. Central to Chapter 5 is how the current use of the LSAT (an artificial barrier) hurts law school diversity efforts. This chapter explores academic research that proposes an alternative approach to merit potentially resulting in greater racial and socioeconomic diversity in law schools.

It is not enough for law schools to adopt practices promoting diversity in isolation. The law firm recruiting model is based on a 20th-century approach that will not position firms to improve their diversity representation. Each year, most firms pursue the top 10–15 percent of students from a small group of law schools. Depending on the class size of the school, this could be 20 to 40 people. The lack of a diverse critical mass in law schools suggests that there are few people of color among this group. Further compounding this situation is that firms compete with each other for the same small group of students at the same schools! It is unrealistic to expect a different recruiting result absent a willingness to make structural changes in the hiring process.

Chapter 6 proposes changes that law firms could make in their hiring, evaluation, and promotion practices based on research in organizational psychology. Like any profession, lawyers must validate their employers' decision to hire them through their work product. And similar to any setting in society, unconscious bias influences the lens through which people treat one another. For example, why are fatality rates higher for black and Hispanic male pedestrians, how does race impact the way referees officiate National Basketball Association games, and how does bias impact financial markets? This chapter provides critical responses to each of these questions to demonstrate the pervasiveness of bias and its impact on critical phases in a law firm attorney's career: work product evaluation, annual performance reviews, partnership consideration, and development of relationships with influential partners and institutional clients.

I don't have all the answers. I don't know all the answers. But I know the current approach is broken due in part to a lack of understanding of how we got here. Context matters. History matters. I am not a historian, but this book uses history to provide context. I ask you to join me on this journey and that we, all of us, work together to figure out how to fix the legal profession's approach to creating a more diverse bar. Thank you.

Sincerely,
Kenneth O.C. Imo

CHAPTER 1

From Harriet Tubman to Hurricane Harvey: The Case for Diversity and Inclusion

For nothing is fixed, forever and forever and forever, it is not fixed; the earth is always shifting, the light is always changing, the sea does not cease to grind down rock. Generations do not cease to be born, and we are responsible to them because we are the only witnesses they have. The sea rises, the light fails, lovers cling to each other, and children cling to us. The moment we cease to hold each other, the sea engulfs us and the light goes out.

–James Baldwin

Introduction

Out of respect and reverence, black folks called her "Moses" and Union officers affectionately dubbed her "general." These were the nicknames given to Harriet Tubman, a diminutive African American woman who escaped slavery to become *the* conductor of the Underground Railroad—a network of abolitionists committed to helping African Americans in the South escape slavery. Tubman's heroics as an abolitionist and freedom fighter are well known; what is less known are her contributions to a decisive military campaign in South Carolina during the Civil War. At a time when states sanctioned the ownership and subjugation of African Americans and before women could vote, white Union officers asked Tubman, a black woman born into slavery, to support the war effort as a strategist and recruiter of men.

According to Jeff W. Grigg's book, *The Combahee River Raid: Harriet Tubman & Lowcountry Liberation*, the Union had to accomplish at least three things to have a successful military campaign in South Carolina: (1) they needed to cripple the plantations by cutting off access to the Combahee River—a major artery for the plantations and Confederate soldiers; (2) because Confederate soldiers outnumbered Union soldiers, they needed to bolster their numbers by recruiting African Americans; and (3) they needed to earn the trust of former enslaved people who, for obvious reasons, did not trust white people.[1] Tubman helped the Union accomplish all three.

Answering the questions "why diversity?" or "what is the business case for diversity?" can be challenging for anyone. People often recite platitudes such as "it is the right thing to do," "we appreciate diversity of thought," "it just makes business sense," or several other similar responses that fail to articulate the importance of this issue to them. While I personally think that diversity makes us better and is one of our nation's strengths, it is necessary to develop a response that is consistent with your and your organization's core values, culture, and business strategy. Forward-thinking organizations define their diversity business case, and can respond adequately and appropriately to challenging and controversial events.

The first part of this chapter uses Harriet Tubman's strategic contributions to the Civil War to address the business case for diversity from a historical military perspective. Union officers' decision to leverage Tubman's unique skill set provides an example of how leaders should proactively look for opportunities to leverage diversity. The second part of the chapter explores diversity as an intangible asset that directly impacts an organization's brand and its bottom line. Examples provided here include the economic impact of the "bathroom bill" on North Carolina's economy, the lingering consequences of the University of Missouri's failure to adequately respond to student concerns of racial animus, and the business and political communities' responses to the white supremacist protests in Charlottesville, Virginia, in August 2017. But first, we will begin with Tubman and the Combahee River Raid.

---

1. Jeff W. Grigg, The Combahee River Raid: Harriet Tubman & Lowcountry Liberation (2014).

Harriet Tubman: Entrepreneur, Abolitionist, Strategist, Leader of Men

Harriet Tubman's entrepreneurial spirit and craving for freedom made her an abolitionist. As a young woman, she convinced her owner to hire herself to other slave owners for a fee that she split with her owner. Tubman used the money to buy oxen for hauling timber, and she eventually expanded her business into farming and doing various jobs at wharfs on the Eastern Shore of Maryland. Tubman's work on the wharfs exposed her to black and white mariners with abolitionist connections in northern port cities. These people also provided her with escape route information and contacts who could be helpful in the event of her escape from slavery.[2]

Tubman undertook her first actions on the Underground Railroad to safeguard against the breakup of her family following the death of her owner. Tubman's initial escape occurred with her two brothers. It was short-lived because they convinced her to return, but a few weeks later she left for good and returned to Maryland only to free relatives and other enslaved people. According to Paul Donnelly's article for the *New York Times*, she led approximately 12 missions that freed more than 100 people, making Tubman a celebrity who would be called upon by prominent abolitionists for the most sensitive operations.[3]

In 1850, the Fugitive Slave Act prohibited northern states from serving as a safe haven for people fleeing slavery. Consequently, it became too dangerous for Tubman to travel south on rescue missions, so she stopped and settled with her family in Canada. Abolitionist John Brown, the would-be leader of a slave revolt in Harpers Ferry, Virginia, went to Canada soliciting her support in recruiting African Americans to assist in his raid. Tubman admired Brown and his cause and encouraged people to join his insurrection. Brown's raid failed and ended in his death, but it marked the first time that a white man asked Tubman to use her gravitas and influence to assist a military campaign. The second would be on a much larger scale with a very different outcome.

Tubman often went to Boston in the years leading up to the Civil War. The city was home to some of the most influential abolitionists, so she used these trips to fundraise for Canada's black community, to earn a living telling

2. *Id.* at 17–18.

3. Paul Donnelly, *Harriet Tubman's Great Raid*, N.Y. Times, June 7, 2013, https://opinionator.blogs.nytimes.com/2013/06/07/harriet-tubmans-great-raid/.

her story, and to cement relationships in Boston's abolitionist community. Tubman developed a friendship with John Andrew, Massachusetts governor and leading abolitionist. Andrew thought she could be an asset to the Civil War effort and recommended that the Union send Tubman to South Carolina to help the Army give aid to thousands of newly freed people. Her initial war service included assisting Union surgeons in treating wounded white soldiers. Tubman's hospital work also gave her opportunities to interact with people fleeing slavery in the Confederacy. These men and women did not trust white Union officers but were more than willing to provide Tubman with information that could hurt the Confederacy's war effort. As more enslaved people escaped, the word spread that they should see "Miss Harriet."[4]

Tubman's role increased as she gained the confidence of and credibility with Union officers who recognized the strategic value of her involvement in the war effort in South Carolina. Tubman accompanied the Union Army as it moved farther inland from coastal South Carolina. She visited liberated slave camps along the coast and recruited ten scouts from those plantations who later helped with a decisive military campaign in South Carolina. Tubman tried to meet every person who escaped slavery to get as much intelligence from them as possible. Union generals insisted that they needed Tubman to get people talking to her, so officers gave her money to pay people for information. She learned how many people were at the plantations and the best routes to access those plantations.[5]

Tubman met Colonel James Montgomery, leader of the newly formed Second South Carolina Volunteers—a group composed mostly of black troops—in February 1863. Montgomery and Tubman shared a connection to John Brown. Montgomery was an abolitionist who fought beside Brown, and Tubman recruited men to join Brown's Harpers Ferry raid. Montgomery was responsible for orchestrating what become known as the Combahee River Raid and worked with Tubman to plan it based on the intelligence she gathered and the soldiers she recruited. Tubman accompanied Montgomery and his men not as a passenger, but as a strategist, a commander of scouts, and an intermediary for black soldiers and white Union officers.

4. GRIGG, *supra* note 1, at 21–22.
5. *Id.*

The Combahee River Raid was a success. Montgomery's Second South Carolina Volunteers knew which routes along the river were most vulnerable to attack. According to Griggs, they methodically destroyed plantations that provided the Confederacy with food, livestock, and supplies without suffering a single casualty. The raid also resulted in the freeing of approximately 800 enslaved men, women, and children by black troops. The operation succeeded in part because military strategists devised a strong plan, they knew what they needed to make it work, they positioned people to succeed, and they were willing to rely on Tubman—a black woman who was a former slave—to develop and lead a team of scouts whose intelligence proved consequential to the operation.[6] Tubman's involvement in the Combahee River Raid exemplifies why diversity is the right thing to do and how it can provide a competitive advantage.

Civil War military operations and law firm management are not quite the same thing, but the leadership lessons are transferable. There are several practical reasons why diversity is good for organizations: it strengthens an organization's brand, research indicates that it has a positive impact on financial markets, and the increased representation of women and people of color on corporate boards is good for business. But the standard response is that diversity is the "right thing to do." While laudatory, it is unrealistic to assume that altruism alone will somehow ensure a level playing field for all lawyers to succeed in big law or for organizations to take proactive measures to develop inclusive environments. Therefore, the willingness of Union officers to see strategic value in Tubman and to empower her to use her knowledge in a mutually beneficial way cannot be understated.

According to "Rethinking the Baseline in Diversity Research: Should We Be Explaining the Effects of Homogeneity?," it is well documented that cognitive diversity—the variety of approaches brought to problem solving by diverse groups—improves business outcomes and prevents groupthink.[7] However, diverse teams may also result in greater conflict when there is a lack of awareness of how to build inclusivity. According to research by psychologists on homophily—the idea that people naturally associate more with people similar

6. *Id.*

7. Evan P. Apfelbaum et al., *Rethinking the Baseline in Diversity Research*, 9 PERSP. ON PSYCHOL. SCI. 235 (2014), *available at* http://pps.sagepub.com/content/9/3/235.

to them, including being similar in race/ethnicity—people are more likely to give opportunities to members of their particular group.[8] Studies have also shown that in-group preferential treatment is a stronger motive driving group conflict than out-group opposition.[9] This preference for in-group members can also manifest in outcomes that may even be harmful to clients.

One example that highlights the detrimental effects of homophily is captured in an article published in the *Proceedings of the National Academy of Sciences of the United States of America*.[10] Researchers selected participants who were randomly assigned to ethnically homogenous and diverse markets. The study revealed that in the homogenous market scenario, traders were more likely to accept speculative prices. Consequently, overpricing was higher and these markets suffered more severe crashes when bubbles burst. In ethnically diverse markets, market prices fit true values 58 percent better than in homogenous markets and, as a result, market crashes were less severe. The researchers concluded that in addition to human errors and economic climate, price bubbles may also be a consequence of the social context of decision making. This is because ethnic diversity may foster friction, resulting in beneficial skepticism. Conversely, a characteristic of homogeneity is overwhelming confidence that translates into a "herd mentality"—which is often associated with pricing bubbles.

Further making this point is an independent evaluation by the International Monetary Fund (IMF) assessing its role in not foreseeing or preventing the global financial crisis. In its evaluation, the IMF attributed its inability to foresee the Great Recession to a "high degree of groupthink, intellectual capture, [and] a general mindset" that large advanced economies could not trigger a major financial crisis.[11]

Slavery and the fight against ending it during the Civil War represent the most blatant forms of homogeneity. But some people managed to rise above this mentality in ways that allowed a former enslaved African American woman to lead men in a military campaign that freed hundreds of other

8. *Id.* at 236.

9. *Id.*

10. Sheen S. Levine et al., *Ethnic Diversity Deflates Price Bubbles*, 111 Proc. Nat'l Acad. Sci. U.S.A. 18524–29 (2014).

11. Independent Evaluation Office of the International Monetary Fund, IMF Performance in the Run-Up to the Financial and Economic Crisis 1 (2011).

people. Today, homogeneity does not manifest itself as it did in the 19th century, but it does exist, and this topic and unconscious bias will be addressed in subsequent chapters. The business case for inclusion is central to the remainder of this chapter. In "Examining the Link between Diversity and Firm Performance: The Effects of Diversity Reputation and Leader Racial Diversity," professors Quinetta M. Roberson and Hyeon Jeong Park state that corporate reputation—how organizations are perceived to create value relative to their competitors—is among the most important intangible business assets.[12] Corporate reputation includes a commitment to diversity and the ability to build and maintain an inclusive environment. The financial implications of North Carolina's bathroom bill, the consequences of the 2015 University of Missouri protests, and business and political communities' reactions to the events that took place in Charlottesville, Virginia, in August 2017 illustrate the link between diversity and inclusion and business.

House Bill 2: The Bathroom Bill That Cost North Carolina Almost $1 Billion

In March 2016, a *Charlotte Observer* article[13] reported that in response to a Charlotte, North Carolina, ordinance extending rights to gay and/or transgender people, the North Carolina state legislature passed a law that went further than reversing the ordinance.[14] The law passed by the North Carolina General Assembly, known as the Public Facilities Privacy and Security Act, HB2, or the Charlotte bathroom bill, made it illegal for cities to expand upon existing laws regulating workplace discrimination, the use of public accommodations, and certain business issues. The law mandated that transgender

12. Quinetta M. Roberson & Hyeon Jeong Park, Examining the Link between Diversity and Firm Performance: The Effects of Diversity Reputation and Leader Racial Diversity (Center for Advanced Human Resource Studies Working Paper #06-02, 2006), *available at* https://digitalcommons.ilr.cornell.edu/cgi/viewcontent.cgi?referer=https://www.bing.com/&httpsredir=1&article=1401&context=cahrswp.

13. Michael Gordon et al., *Understanding HB2: North Carolina's Newest Law Solidifies State's Role in Defining Discrimination*, Charlotte Observer, Mar. 26, 2016, http://www.charlotteobserver.com/news/politics-government/article68401147.html.

14. *Id.*

people use public restrooms in accordance with the gender on their birth certificates and nullified local ordinances that extended protections to the LGBT community.

The business community's reaction was intense:

- Protests by companies and performers resulted in the cancellation of business expansions and entertainment events.
- On July 21, the National Basketball Association (NBA) moved its All-Star Game from Charlotte in 2017, which cost the city approximately $100 million.
- In September 2016, the National Collegiate Athletic Association (NCAA) removed seven championships scheduled to be held in North Carolina during the 2016–2017 academic year, including two rounds of the wildly popular men's basketball tournament.
- Two days later, the Atlantic Coast Conference (ACC) announced that it would remove the ACC football championship game in December from Charlotte in protest of the law.
- Large businesses including Bank of America, Dow Chemical, and Wells Fargo demanded repeal.
- Despite pushback from the business community, Governor Pat McCrory dug in and in November 2016 lost his reelection bid to Attorney General Roy Cooper—which political observers attributed to the governor's support of HB2.[15]
- In March 2017, *Politico* reported that North Carolina suffered an estimated $630 million in lost revenue.[16]

In March 2017, North Carolina's Democratic Governor Roy Cooper and the Republican-led state legislature reached a compromise to ease some of the restrictions of HB2. A March 29, 2017, *New York Times* article quoted Governor Cooper as saying, "I support the House Bill 2 repeal compromise . . . It's not a perfect deal, but it repeals House Bill 2 and begins to repair our

15. *Id.*

16. Elena Schneider, *The Bathroom Bill That Ate North Carolina*, Politico, Mar. 23, 2017, https://www.politico.com/magazine/story/2017/03/the-bathroom-bill-that-ate-north-carolina-214944.

reputation."[17] In September 2017, the *Los Angeles Times* published an Associated Press article reporting that Credit Suisse announced it would expand its presence in North Carolina by 1,200 jobs because of the repeal of HB2, and the NBA reversed course and awarded the 2019 All-Star Game to Charlotte.[18]

The University of Missouri: Protests, Resignations, Damaged Reputations, Lost Revenue

According to a November 9, 2015, article in the *Slatest*, historically it has been challenging for the University of Missouri to address race and diversity issues.[19] In 2001, the university hired a chief diversity officer and attempted to include a diversity course in the school's curriculum based on a campus-wide survey to gauge attitudes on diversity and inclusion. Diversity efforts stalled in 2010, and issues roared back five years later in ways that damaged the University of Missouri's reputation and resulted in the resignations of high-level officials.

The fall of 2015 brought forth a tumultuous year for the University of Missouri. On August 14, 2015, graduate students received less than 24 hours' notice that the university would cut their health care.[20] The decision resulted in a rally, a list of demands, and a graduate student walkout that would serve as an ominous sign of things to come a few weeks later when the university failed to respond adequately to students' concerns about racism.

In September, Missouri Students Association President Payton Head brought national attention to the university's deteriorating campus climate when he spoke publicly about his experience with racism on campus. Approximately two weeks after Head's comments, students held the first of three

17. Richard Fausset, *North Carolina Strikes a Deal to Repeal Restrictive Bathroom Law*, N.Y. Times, Mar. 29, 2017, https://www.nytimes.com/2017/03/29/us/north-carolina-lawmakers-reach-deal-to-repeal-so-called-bathroom-bill.html.

18. Associated Press, *Lawsuit Says North Carolina "Bathroom Bill" Effects Still Felt*, L.A. Times, July 21, 2017, http://www.latimes.com/nation/nationnow/la-na-nc-bathroom-bill-lawsuit-20170721-story.html.

19. Claire Landsbaum & Greta Weber, *What Happened at the University of Missouri?*, Slatest, Nov. 9, 2015, http://www.slate.com/blogs/the_slatest/2015/11/09/timeline_of_u_of_missouri_protests_and_president_resignation.html.

20. Sarah Sabatke, *University of Missouri Students Protest to Highlight Racial Inequality*, Huffington Post, Dec. 6, 2017, https://www.huffingtonpost.com/sarah-sabatke/university-of-missouri-protests_b_8502334.html.

"Racism Lives Here" rallies criticizing the administration's delayed response to reported racial incidents. Tensions only seemed to rise because more incidents ensued. On October 5, members of the university's Legion of Black Collegians' Homecoming Royal Court were harassed and called racial slurs during rehearsal for a homecoming play. On the heels of that incident someone drew a swastika in feces in a dorm bathroom—the second anti-Semitic incident in a residence hall in the past year.

And, just hours after students confronted University of Missouri System President Tim Wolfe at a homecoming parade about perceived inadequate response to concerns related to persistent racism on campus, white students called two black students "nigger" outside of the student recreation complex at the University of Missouri campus.[21]

According to the *Slatest*, on November 7, 2015, University of Missouri football players announced in a tweet that they would boycott all practices and games "until President Tim Wolfe resigns or is removed due to his negligence toward marginalized students' experiences." The following day, the University of Missouri Head Football Coach Gary Pinkel showed support for players when he tweeted a group photo of the team that said: "The Mizzou Family stands as one. We are united. We are behind our players."[22] This stance by the football team could have resulted in a $1 million fine for the university had the team forfeited the upcoming football game.

Local and federal politicians weighed in the following day. Two Republican lawmakers demanded that President Tim Wolfe resign, and Democratic Senator Claire McCaskill issued the following statement:

> At this point I think it is essential that the University of Missouri's Board of Curators send a clear message to the students at Mizzou that there is an unqualified commitment to address racism on campus . . . [and] that my university can and will do better in supporting an environment of tolerance and inclusion.[23]

21. Landsbaum & Weber, *supra* note 19.
22. *Id.*
23. *Id.*

On November 10, University of Missouri System President Tim Wolfe resigned and Chancellor R. Bowen Loftin stepped down shortly after. Days before their resignations, both leaders expressed concerns about the campus climate and support for student protestors, but it was too little and too late. The perceived lack of responsiveness, lack of empathy, and inaction cost them their jobs and damaged the University of Missouri's reputation.

Anemona Hartocollis wrote a *New York Times* article detailing the consequences of the protests two years later.[24] Freshmen enrollment at the university's main campus declined by 35 percent from 2015 to 2017, with significant declines among white and black students at 21 percent and 42 percent, respectively. And the drop in white students has been most fiscally damaging because they far outnumber other groups on campus. Before the protests, the university experienced steady growth, but it now faces financial challenges. The lost tuition resulted in budget cuts, there has been a decrease in state funding, the university closed dormitories temporarily, and it cut more than 400 positions.

University officials attribute the enrollment decline to what occurred in 2015. Current University of Missouri System President Mun Choi said, "The general consensus was that it was because of the aftermath of what happened in November 2015. There were students from both in state and out of state that just did not apply, or those who did apply but decided not to attend."[25] Because the university attracts mostly regional students, college admissions counselors believe that it will take several years for the University of Missouri to recover from the consequences of the protests.

Charlottesville

On a Friday evening in mid-August 2017, when many people were engaged in the rituals that accompany the traditions of summertime in our nation, a group of white supremacists descended on Charlottesville to march through the University of Virginia campus in a torchlight procession invoking images

24. Anemona Hartocollis, *Long after Protests, Students Shun the University of Missouri*, N.Y. Times, July 9, 2017, https://www.nytimes.com/2017/07/09/us/university-of-missouri-enrollment-protests-fallout.html.

25. *Id.*

of the Hitler Youth and the Ku Klux Klan (KKK). According to Joe Heim's article for the *Washington Post*, the Friday march included approximately 250 young white men in khaki pants and polo shirts chanting "blood and soil!," "you will not replace us!," "Jews will not replace us," "white lives matter!," and making monkey noises at counterprotesters.[26] Friday's march resulted in shoves, punches, the spraying of chemical irritants, and the marchers throwing their torches at counterprotesters. But each of these acts would pale in comparison to what occurred the following day.

Saturday's rally was scheduled to begin at noon in Emancipation Park in Charlottesville. Rallygoers began converging on the park at 8:00 a.m. chanting slogans, waving nationalist banners, and carrying shields, clubs, and in many cases guns. Counterprotesters also arrived early, many armed with sticks and shields. In addition to the white supremacists (rallygoers) and counterprotesters, armed citizens referred to as a militia also inserted themselves into the day's events. According to Virginia Secretary of Public Safety and Homeland Security Brian Moran, the militia did not appear to be there to cause trouble, but more firearms in that environment was a potential recipe for disaster and confusion because the militia could easily be mistaken for the National Guard.

Things got out of control when rallygoers failed to comply with a previously agreed-upon plan with the Charlottesville Police Department separating them from counterprotesters. Violence ensued as the groups came into contact. Sticks were swung; chemicals were sprayed; and rocks, bottles, and punches were thrown. To quell the violence, the Commonwealth of Virginia declared an unlawful assembly at 11:22 a.m., which appeared to work because the crowd began to disperse. But two hours later, the events of the day took a fatal turn when rallygoer James Alex Fields, Jr. drove his car into a crowd of pedestrians, killing Heather Heyer of Charlottesville and injuring 19 others.

Condemnation of the violence in Charlottesville was immediate and bipartisan, and many unequivocally blamed the white supremacists. However, President Donald J. Trump initially blamed both sides for the violence

26. Joe Heim, *Recounting a Day of Rage, Hate, Violence, and Death*, Wash. Post, Aug. 14, 2017, https://www.washingtonpost.com/graphics/2017/local/charlottesville-timeline/?utm_term=.85813dd60795.

without condemning white nationalists, then he later condemned white nationalists in prepared remarks, and finally in a press conference he reverted back to his initial comments but added that some of the white nationalists were fine people. Political and business leaders reacted immediately to the president's remarks. Three chief executive officers announced their resignations from the president's manufacturing-advisory council.

A *Weekly Standard* article chronicled Republican policymakers' reactions to the president:

- Senator Cory Gardner of Colorado: "This is nothing short of domestic terrorism & should be named as such."
- Senator Ben Sasse of Nebraska: "These people are utterly revolting—and have no understanding of America."
- Senator Tim Scott of South Carolina: "Domestic terror in #Charlottesville must be condemned by every.single.one.of.us. Otherwise hate is simply emboldened."
- Senator Chuck Grassley of Iowa: "What 'White Natjonalists' are doing in Charlottesville is homegrown terrorism that can't be tolerated anymore that what Any extremist does" [sic throughout].
- Senator Ted Cruz of Texas: "The Nazis, the KKK, and white supremacists are repulsive and evil, and all of us have a moral obligation to speak out against the lies, bigotry, antiSemitism, and hatred that they propagate."
- Senator Tom Cotton of Arkansas: "These contemptible little men do not speak for what is just, noble, and best about America. They ought to face what they would deny their fellow citizens: the full extent of the law."[27]

The willingness of Republican elected officials to publicly separate themselves from the leader of their party in a political climate rife with partisanship demonstrates the magnitude of the events in Charlottesville. And the reaction of chief executives on the president's manufacturing-advisory council shows

27. Michael Warren, *White House Watch: Trump's Charlottesville Fallout*, WKLY. STANDARD, Aug. 14, 2017, http://www.weeklystandard.com/white-house-watch-trumps-charlottesville-fallout/article/2009273.

the importance to the business community of an unequivocal response to reprehensible behavior by groups such as the white supremacists in Charlottesville. Business leaders were so taken aback by the absence of a full-throated condemnation of racial strife by the president that they chose not to associate themselves or their businesses with council, thwarting the goal of helping the manufacturing industry.

A *Wall Street Journal* article referenced reasons the following CEOs gave for resigning from the manufacturing-advisory council:

- Merck Chairman and CEO Kenneth Frazier said the following when he announced his resignation: "America's leaders must honor our fundamental values by clearly rejecting expressions of hatred, bigotry and group supremacy, which run counter to the American ideal that all people are created equal . . . As CEO of Merck and as a matter of personal conscience, I feel a responsibility to take a stand against intolerance and extremism."
- Intel Corp. CEO Brian Krzanich said he resigned "to call attention to the serious harm our divided political climate is causing to critical issues," and to condemn "white supremacists and their ilk who marched and committed violence."
- In announcing his resignation, Under Armour Inc. Founder and CEO Kevin Plank said, "We are saddened by #Charlottesville. There is no place for racism or discrimination in this world. We choose love & unity."[28]

Conclusion: Hurricane Harvey and Human Chains

In August 2017, Hurricane Harvey ravaged the Texas Gulf Coast when it brought 50 inches of rain, resulting in dozens of deaths, damaged homes and businesses, and human loss and sorrow existing long after the water receded.[29] Events in our nation over the past several years reveal fissures that exist when

28. Peter Loftus, *Three CEOs Quit Trump Advisory Council after Charlottesville Violence*, Wall St. J., Aug. 15, 2017, https://www.wsj.com/articles/merck-ceo-quits-trump-advisory-council-after-charlottesville-violence-1502717371.

29. *Historic Hurricane Harvey's Recap*, Weather Channel, Sept. 2, 2017, https://weather.com/storms/hurricane/news/tropical-storm-harvey-forecast-texas-louisiana-arkansas#/!.

we are pitted against each other. But we should try to find inspiration in the response to Hurricane Harvey.

Interwoven in the images of destruction and human sorrow were acts of kindness and cooperation transcending the tribalism that pulls us apart. That spirit of connectedness we witnessed in the tragedy on the Texas Gulf Coast—one of the most diverse regions in the nation—represents the essence and power of diversity and inclusion. One such example was a group of strangers that formed a human chain to rescue an elderly man from a truck submerged in flood waters. Had any of those people stopped to think about their political affiliations, religious beliefs, race, and so on, the man may have drowned. Diversity is important because it makes us better when we do not approach it as a zero-sum game but as something that expands opportunity for everyone.

Harriet Tubman's involvement in the Civil War exemplifies how benefits from diversity and inclusion extend beyond an individual. Tubman had an opportunity to contribute meaningfully to a cause that benefited former enslaved people, the Union Army, and the nation. Recent history—from the passage of the bathroom bill in North Carolina, the reactions to the response of the University of Missouri administrators to racist incidents, and the aftermath of Charlottesville—demonstrates the importance of diversity and inclusion to business leaders, students, and ordinary citizens. It is incumbent upon institutions to get these issues right because brands, reputations, and revenue are at stake, and the focus on diversity and inclusion is not going anywhere.

An obvious question: how do we approach something as complex as valuing difference and leveling the playing field for opportunity when the field has been inherently uneven? The next chapter will answer this question by examining steps Branch Rickey took to orchestrate the integration of Major League Baseball when Jackie Robinson became the first African American to play in the big leagues.

CHAPTER 2

Branch Rickey and the Integration of Professional Baseball: Courageous, Empathetic Leadership Matters

One is a majority if he is right.

–President Abraham Lincoln

Introduction

It is April 15 and the Major League Baseball (MLB) season is underway. But this day is different; it is Jackie Robinson Day and every player, coach, and manager on both teams wears the number 42 to commemorate and honor Jackie Robinson. On April 15, 1947, Robinson propelled the nation forward when he took the field as a Brooklyn Dodger to become the first African American MLB player. Robinson integrated the national pastime—a sport revered by all Americans but reserved only for white players at the highest level. Since 2004, MLB rightfully acknowledges Robinson as one of the sport's heroes, but honoring Robinson without mentioning Branch Rickey leaves the story incomplete.

Breaking MLB's entrenched color barrier was hard. The U.S. Supreme Court made segregation the law in 1896 in *Plessy v. Ferguson*.[1] It codified a racial caste system with African Americans solidly at the bottom in every facet of life—including which restrooms and water fountains people used, how the

1. Plessy v. Ferguson, 163 U.S. 537 (1896).

nation educated black and white children, and even who could play baseball at the highest level. Racism was the norm and challenging it could result in loss of life, limb, and livelihood. Robinson risked being a victim of all three as the first black man to play major league baseball, and anyone who helped him also had a lot to lose. Branch Rickey, the architect behind integrating baseball, took this risk when he challenged the prevailing social norms of the country.

Robinson was an extraordinary person: he was a multisport athlete at the University of California, Los Angeles, he served the nation as an Army second lieutenant in World War II, and he excelled as a professional baseball player in the Negro Leagues. But Robinson may not have been the best player in the Negro Leagues. Because segregation barred African Americans from playing major league baseball, the best black players starred in the Negro Leagues, where Rickey discovered Robinson. This all-black league featured several African Americans who could have played in the MLB. The problem was not a shortage of talented black athletes, but that there were few Branch Rickeys—powerful white men who saw the immorality, injustice, and business loss in racism.

Integrating baseball involved confronting the baseball establishment, a cadre of rich owners beholden to Judge Kenesaw Mountain Landis, the first MLB commissioner. According to David Pietrusza in *Judge and Jury: The Life and Times of Judge Kenesaw Mountain Landis*, his parents named him after the Battle of Kennesaw Mountain, one of the worst defeats for the Union during the Civil War. His father, a Union doctor, suffered a terrible wound that almost cost him his leg. Judge Landis was aptly named because he *was* the baseball establishment and an immovable obstacle to integrating baseball. Rickey's quest to integrate baseball meant contending with the Mountain and the other keepers of MLB's grip on segregation.[2]

The furtherance of diversity and inclusion requires empathy, humility, and the willingness to use power: empathy to stand in the shoes of someone whose life experiences may be vastly different from yours and viewing those differences as opportunities and not obstacles; the humility to know you may not have all the answers, and possessing the curiosity to seek them out; and the awareness of power—your own and the institution you represent—and

2. David Pietrusza, Judge and Jury: The Life and Times of Judge Kenesaw Mountain Landis 17 (1998).

the willingness to use power to level a playing field tilted in a way that does not ensure equal opportunity for everyone based solely on merit. Branch Rickey's role in integrating baseball is relevant because it represents the convergence of all three: empathy, humility, and power.

The Vanishing Black Baseball Player

According to Roger Kahn, author of *Rickey & Robinson: The True, Untold Story of the Integration of Baseball*, enslaved African Americans began playing baseball in the 1830s.[3] The sport became the national pastime after the Civil War, with the emergence of several amateur and professional leagues. A strong desire to prevent African Americans from playing the game accompanied its burgeoning popularity. In 1868 (five years after the Emancipation Proclamation and three years after the Civil War ended), the National Association of Base Ball Players—the precursor to the MLB—banned teams from its league with "one or more colored persons."[4]

In the 1870s, baseball matured from an amateur, club sport into a professional endeavor. With this maturation came the splintering of the National Association into competing organizations fielding their own professional teams. These teams were not beholden to the 1868 racist ban, so African Americans briefly played professional baseball from 1878–1884. Moses Fleetwood Walker and his brother were the first African Americans to play major league baseball. A white pitcher on Walker's team described Walker as the "best catcher he ever worked with," but disliked having a "Negro catcher" so he ignored Walker's pitch signals and threw whatever he wanted.[5] Despite being ignored by his pitcher, Walker still caught anything thrown his way—which was no easy feat.

The Walker brothers both had good seasons, but they were not invited back to their teams the following year. White players, managers, team owners, and the National Association did not want African Americans in the game. As a result, professional baseball abruptly banished black players in 1885, and

3. Roger Kahn, Rickey & Robinson: The True, Untold Story of the Integration of Baseball 17–19 (2014).

4. *Id.* at 19.

5. *Id.*

within 15 years they were gone from the minor leagues too. Unlike in 1868, there was no official public decree announcing a ban of black players; they simply vanished. And an official ban was unnecessary because in 1896 the U.S. Supreme Court essentially followed the lead of professional baseball in *Plessy v. Ferguson*[6] by declaring "separate but equal" constitutional.

The Mountain

The man who would become the first and arguably the most powerful commissioner in MLB history was born in Millville, Ohio, in 1866 to a "highly visible, idea-oriented and flamboyant" family.[7] His father served the Union during the Civil War, and his four older brothers succeeded in journalism and politics, with two serving as elected officials in the U.S. House of Representatives. Landis also pursued a life in public service but without running for office. In 1891, he settled in Chicago after gaining admission to the Illinois Bar, and got as a mentor Walter Quintin Gresham, who would eventually introduce Landis to another mentor, President Grover Cleveland.

According to Pietrusza, Gresham was one of the most influential people in the country in the decades following the Civil War. He served in three separate cabinet posts and was considered a viable presidential candidate, and he was a Landis family friend. In 1893, President Cleveland named Gresham his secretary of state, and Gresham selected Landis as his personal secretary. While in Washington, Landis ingratiated himself with press members, Gresham, and Gresham's influential circle of friends to include President Cleveland. Gresham presciently said of Landis to Cleveland, "[S]ome day when you and I are forgotten he will be known as one of the great men of all time."[8]

Landis's connections gained from his time in Washington would serve him well. He returned to Chicago and opened a successful law firm with two former Washington associates (a former ambassador to Germany and the former assistant postmaster general).[9] He also inserted himself into the Chicago political scene as an influential Republican despite having served in a

6. *Plessy*, 163 U.S. 537.
7. Pietrusza, *supra* note 2, at 3.
8. *Id.* at 17–23.
9. *Id.* at 29.

Democratic administration. In 1904, Landis was the campaign manager for Frank Orren Lowden's first unsuccessful run for Illinois governor. Despite the loss, President Theodore Roosevelt held Lowden in high regard and accepted Lowden's recommendation to name his good friend, Kenesaw Mountain Landis, to a judgeship on the U.S. District Court for the Northern District of Illinois. In 1905, at 39 years old, Landis became a federal judge, and two years later he would preside over a case that would transform the American business landscape forever.

President Roosevelt took office in 1903, determined to bring down the nation's largest companies that had a knack for stifling competition, propelling prices, and making profits exceeding fair market levels. Congress passed the Sherman Antitrust Act in 1890 to combat these companies, but it was Roosevelt, nicknamed the "Trust Buster," who initiated a frontal assault against monopolies when his administration brought more than 50 lawsuits against the largest monopolies. The largest monopoly was Standard Oil Company owned by John D. Rockefeller. Standard Oil controlled 85 percent of the nation's refined oil, and in 1907 it found itself in federal court before Judge Landis, facing a 1,462-count indictment. The jury found Standard Oil guilty on all counts and Judge Landis imposed the largest fine ever for an American court, $29,240,000. The decision made Landis a legal legend and someone not to be trifled with, as major league baseball would discover a few years later when Landis would preside over an even higher-profile case involving the national pastime.[10]

Landis, an avid baseball fan, had the good fortune to preside over two of organized baseball's most consequential cases, which ultimately positioned him to become the first MLB commissioner. The first case involved the newly formed Federal League (Feds), which challenged the American League (organized baseball's predominant league) by establishing franchises in several competing markets, resulting in the defections of American League players to the Feds for higher salaries. What ensued was a protracted battle between the two leagues, resulting in an antitrust lawsuit brought by the Feds in Judge Landis's court. The Feds assumed Landis, who had a reputation for being a

10. *Id.* at 47–50.

"trust buster," would be sympathetic to their cause. The Feds, however, did not know that Landis feared a decision in the case would hurt baseball.[11]

During the trial, Landis asked the litigants, "[D]o you realize that the decision in this case may tear down the very foundation of this game, so loved by thousands . . .?"[12] Landis chose to do nothing. The season began and ended without a verdict. The American League bought out the Feds and Landis dismissed the case one year after hearing it. Landis's intentional delay tactics saved organized baseball and made the owners indebted to him—which Landis cashed in on later after being called upon to rescue baseball again.

A gambling scandal tainted the outcome of the 1919 World Series. Experts favored the Chicago White Sox to beat the Cincinnati Reds, but the Reds won in eight games.[13] People suspected the fix was in. And in 1920, it was revealed that eight White Sox players, gamblers, and mobsters colluded to throw the series. The scandal rocked the public trust in the integrity of major league baseball.[14] The owners concluded that someone with gravitas and a public persona demanding respect should lead baseball. The owners considered several high-profile people—former President William Howard Taft, General John J. Pershing, Senator Hiram Johnson (R-Cal.), presidential contender General Leonard Wood, former Treasury Secretary (and Woodrow Wilson's son-in-law) William Gibbs McAdoo, and Judge Landis. The owners decided Landis fit the bill, and a group of them wanted to tell him in person at the federal courthouse where Landis was hearing a case. During this initial encounter, Landis immediately set the tone for how he would work with the owners and, by extension, govern baseball.

Landis made the most powerful men in baseball wait 45 minutes before acknowledging their presence; he ordered them to be quiet as they began talking among themselves at the back of the courtroom during his trial; and when they offered Landis the position (which he expected them to do), he extracted concessions from them that made him the most powerful person in sports. The owners vowed to never publicly criticize Landis, they agreed to be bound by his decisions and to never challenge them in court, and, according

11. *Id.* at 153–55.
12. *Id.* at 157.
13. *Id.* at 162.
14. *Id.* at 169–70.

to Pietrusza, they signed an unprecedented oath of fealty that said the following: "We . . . hereby pledge ourselves loyally to support the Commissioner . . . assure him that each of us will acquiesce in his decisions even when we believe them mistaken and that we will not discredit the sport by public criticism of him and of one another."[15]

In 1920, Judge Landis became the MLB commissioner with unfettered powers, positioning him to be either a facilitator of racial integration, or the biggest obstacle to anyone even contemplating the entry of African Americans into organized baseball. He was the latter and remained so until his death in 1944. Rickey's experiment to integrate baseball contended with a deep-seated racism excluding black ball players as far back as the 1880s and with the Mountain, an establishment figure deeply committed to preserving the traditions of baseball—a sport owned, managed, coached, and played exclusively by white men. Rickey had other ideas and had to call upon his sense of morality, fairness, justice, and understanding of the baseball culture and business.

Branch Rickey

The man who became the architect of baseball's Great Experiment showed no signs of being one of the country's great social engineers. Wesley Branch Rickey was born December 20, 1881, to a deeply religious family in rural Ohio 15 years before *Plessy* and just three years before the Walker brothers integrated professional baseball for the first time with the Toledo Blue Stockings. After completing grade school, he worked on the family farm, but his parents knew he would not have a future in manual labor because Rickey was a voracious reader and avid talker. Instead of farming, Rickey contributed to the household and saved for college by earning a certificate that allowed him to teach before completing high school. He eventually saved enough money to attend Ohio Wesleyan University.[16]

Rickey's college experience put him on a circuitous path that involved playing and coaching college, semiprofessional, and minor league baseball. But two experiences as a college baseball coach aroused empathy and shaped his views on the injustice of racism and the need for deliberate action. Both

15. *Id.* at 173–74.
16. Lee Lowenfish, Branch Rickey: Baseball's Ferocious Gentleman 14 (2009).

incidents involved Charles "Tommy" Thomas, the only African American on Rickey's team and one of the few black students at Ohio Wesleyan University. In 1903, in a road game against the University of Kentucky, in response to a group of white fans chanting "get that nigger off the field," Rickey, a 21-year-old head coach, threatened to remove his entire team from the field if Thomas could not play.[17]

The other incident involved Thomas being denied entry into the team hotel in South Bend, Indiana, for a game against Notre Dame University. Rickey refused to split up his team, so he demanded to see the hotel manager whom he convinced to put a cot in his room where Thomas could sleep. The demeaning experience left Thomas hurt, and that evening in their hotel room Rickey watched as Thomas sobbed and scratched at his body as if to remove his black skin. Both experiences gave Rickey perspective and conjured feelings of empathy that would motivate him to rid baseball of the injustices of racism when he had the influence to do so. But he first had to embark on a middling playing career that eventually evolved into him becoming a visionary baseball executive.

From 1905–1914, he had a sporadic career with the St. Louis Browns resulting in 120 appearances. Between playing, coaching, and doing a host of other odd jobs, Rickey graduated from the University of Michigan Law School in 1911. He became a sole practitioner in Boise, Idaho, and described his short legal career a miserable failure because he had one client who did not even want a lawyer. Fortunately, he made a good enough impression as a coach and player and spent his summers in Boise scouting baseball players for St. Louis Browns' owner Robert Hedges. Hedges found Rickey to be intelligent and articulate and offered him a full-time position to serve a quasi-role as scout and general manager. As a player, Rickey's career was undistinguished, but his tenure in the Browns' front office made him an unrivaled evaluator of talent.

In 1912, during his first few months with the team, the Browns drafted one-third of the players recommended by Rickey—no small feat.[18] In 1913, Rickey correctly identified 30 of the 108 minor league players selected by the 16 MLB teams that season. Rickey so impressed Hedges that before the end of 1913, he asked Rickey to become the field manager in addition to vice

17. *Id.* at 22–23.
18. *Id.* at 63.

president, business manager, and chief developer of talent, all at the age of 32. As a field manager, Rickey inspired his players with lectures and heartfelt motivational speeches—all of which would serve him well 30 years later in his pursuit to integrate baseball. Rickey showed early signs of being a baseball innovator by introducing statistical analysis to games by keeping track of how many bases each player made himself and those that advanced his teammates.

Rickey left the Browns organization in 1918 to be the president of the St. Louis Cardinals. Initially, it was a terrible job. The organization was financially strapped, the team was awful, and Rickey had a bad relationship with his field manager. But Rickey seized this opportunity to make the Cardinals relevant for a generation, while revolutionizing baseball in the process. Shortly after joining the organization, he left the team to serve in the Army during World War I. He found the team in worse financial shape when he returned in December of that year. Out of necessity, he made several changes demonstrating keen acumen as a baseball executive and innovator. To cut costs, Rickey made himself the field manager while continuing to oversee front office operations. He was much better at being a front office executive and deserves credit for creating the modern office of baseball business manager. Because the Cardinals were not very good, it was difficult to compete with the better teams for minor league talent. So Rickey created the farm system—a chain of minor-league teams solely owned by the Cardinals. This enabled the Cardinals to circumvent the existing system by giving them early access to players they could sign, keep the best ones, contend for championships, and become a lucrative franchise.[19]

Rickey's plan worked, and the Cardinals thrived, winning nine pennants and six World Series from 1926–1946. Rickey, without question, possessed one of the greatest minds in baseball. He was an astute judge of talent and masterful at running the Cardinals' business, but he also acquired his detractors along the way. Judge Landis was one of them. According to Kahn, Landis despised the farm system, what he described as Rickey's "covetous acquisition" of young players.[20] In 1938, Landis unilaterally released all of the St. Louis Cardinals farm system players, resulting in a loss of talent for the Cardinals

19. *Id.* at 82.
20. Kahn, *supra* note 3, at 5.

and the potential end of Rickey's career years before he broke baseball's color barrier.[21]

Despite Landis's dismantling of the farm system, Rickey cemented his baseball bona fides in St. Louis. He developed a reputation as a shrewd executive, motivational speaker, friend of politicians, and was even encouraged to run for governor of Missouri. Despite his stature, Rickey showed no signs of integrating baseball during his tenure with the Cardinals. The entire organization was white, from the players to the scouts, coaches, and managers. When asked about this years later, Rickey said his time in St. Louis did not present the best circumstances for integration. Cardinals' ownership was not interested in it and Rickey described St. Louis as a southern city dominated by whites and where blacks "hid" in corners. "You can only make a bold move when the time and place are right," Rickey said.[22] In 1942, the timing and location were right when Rickey left the St. Louis Cardinals to become the general manager of the Brooklyn Dodgers.

The Path to Integration

Rickey embarked on his plan to integrate baseball immediately after joining the Dodgers. He combined motives and methods to pursue black players. His belief in fairness, his perception of baseball as a microcosm of society, and his desire to win and draw fans (Brooklyn had a significant black population at the time) motivated him. Rickey also knew that he had to find a player who possessed a combination of baseball talent, maturity, and an extraordinary amount of self-discipline because that player would endure an unconscionable level of scrutiny fueled by a deep-seated racism resistant to the mere thought of a black man playing the nation's pastime at the highest level.[23]

Rickey began his mission by casting a broad net in scouting players of color and sought help from several people. However, only his family knew his true intention was to break MLB's color barrier. Rickey considered Latin American countries to be the major source of talent. He asked a fraternity brother to look for players in South America, enlisted another friend

21. *Id.* at 6.
22. *Id.* at 76.
23. Lowenfish, *supra* note 16, at 349.

in identifying Puerto Rican players, and he sent one of his best scouts to Mexico to evaluate a prospect. During World War II, black and white baseball players played each other in wartime exhibition games between Negro League and MLB athletes. Rickey sent scouts to these games to draft reports on every player.[24]

Rickey appreciated that integrating baseball could not occur in a vacuum; it was part of the nation's struggle with human rights, so he studied the issues and took a keen interest in current affairs. He saw opportunity in the nation's burgeoning civil rights movement whereby people of color sought equal rights. For example, in 1941, President Franklin D. Roosevelt signed an executive order banning discrimination in government hiring to prevent a threatened march on Washington, D.C., 20 years before the demonstration led by Dr. Martin Luther King, Jr. To gain additional understanding of the injustices of segregation, Rickey read *An American Dilemma*,[25] a study on race in America published in 1944 that detailed how whites failed to apply their belief in equality and democracy to African Americans. Rickey also knew that as African Americans served the country in World War II to fight against an enemy who peddled the superiority of the white race, it became harder to justify racial discrimination in the United States. This hypocrisy embarrassed the war effort and was indefensible and, consequently, unsustainable.[26]

Despite these factors, many obstacles to the integration of baseball remained. One glaring obstacle was the Mountain himself, Commissioner Landis, the man who forced owners to pledge an oath of fealty to him as a condition for taking the position. Just as Landis undid the Cardinals' farm system, he could have reversed MLB's color ban by decree, but he did not. Baseball owners presented another obstacle. Most of them did not share Rickey's views on racial justice, but they also benefitted financially from segregated baseball. According to Lee Lowenfish, author of *Branch Rickey: The Ferocious Gentleman*, many owners rented their stadiums to Negro League teams when their MLB teams were on the road. This arrangement resulted in earnings of approximately $100,000 in fees for owners.[27] The commissioner, prevailing

24. *Id.* at 349–50.

25. Gunnar Myrdal, An American Dilemma: The Negro Problem and Modern Democracy (1944).

26. Lowenfish, *supra* note 16, at 351–52.

27. *Id.* at 352.

attitudes of segregation, and financial interests were significant hurdles. But Rickey would receive two lucky breaks.

On November 25, 1944, Commissioner Landis died at age 78.[28] Publicly, Rickey praised Landis for restoring the public's trust in baseball following the 1919 World Series scandal. In private, he thought fate removed a big obstacle to integration because he was convinced that Landis would have scuttled his effort to break the color barrier. But Rickey knew Landis's death was not enough because many owners were not interested in challenging the existing racial hierarchy. Rickey believed change drove a successful capitalist system and the end of the war would create opportunities for black players, but he needed an impetus to get things moving. This came with legislation, Rickey's second fortuitous break. On March 13, 1945, the New York State Assembly passed the Ive-Quinn Law. It established the New York State Commission against Discrimination and imposed a $500 fine or one-year jail term on employers refusing to hire anyone based on race.[29]

Rickey now had everything he needed, and after scouting several black and Latino players, he signed Jackie Robinson to a minor league contract with the Montreal Royals in 1946. Robinson's signing with the Royals was an interim step before breaking MLB's color barrier the following year. According to Kahn, in a three-hour meeting before Robinson became a Royal, Rickey prepared Robinson for what he would endure as the first black man to integrate baseball. He told Robinson: "We've got no army. There is virtually nobody on our side. No owners, no umpires, very few newspapermen. And I am afraid that many fans will be hostile." And at a certain point during the conversation, Robinson asked Rickey if he wanted someone who had the courage to fight back. Rickey's response: "I am looking for someone with the courage *not* to fight back."[30]

On April 15, 1947, Robinson broke MLB's color barrier when he made his debut with the Brooklyn Dodgers. There were many talented black baseball players since the imposition of the ban in the 1880s until Robinson's entry into the league, but there were no baseball executives with the courage and vision to give African Americans the opportunity to compete at the

28. *Id.* at 358.

29. *Id.* at 359.

30. Kahn, *supra* note 3, at 107.

highest level. Rickey, president and general manager of the Brooklyn Dodgers, demonstrated courageous visionary leadership when he sought to become the first and only baseball executive to challenge baseball's unwritten rule of barring African American baseball players. The problem was not that there were not enough talented black athletes, the problem was that there were no white executives and owners willing to let them earn their way into the MLB.

Rickey also knew that entry alone was not enough; Robinson had to succeed and doing so in isolation would be difficult if not impossible. Consequently, Rickey immediately became a friend of and advocate for Robinson after signing him. He brought in private coaches to shore up any weaknesses in Robinson's game, and he persuaded the team announcer to set aside his racial bias and to be impartial in evaluating Robinson's play. When a group of white Dodgers players threatened to leave the organization if Robinson signed, Rickey personally intervened to thwart their revolt. Rickey's deliberate actions laid the foundation for Robinson's individual success and the team's success.

Conclusion

Jackie Robinson had a great career and was later inducted into the Baseball Hall of Fame, and the Brooklyn Dodgers became one of the most dominant teams of the 20th century, winning five pennants in eight years, according to Bryan Soderholm-Difatte, author of *The Golden Era of Major League Baseball: A Time of Transition and Integration.* And as Rickey predicted, other teams wanted a piece of the success and also pursued black players, but not all of them were as thoughtful as Rickey and the Dodgers. They all wanted the next Jackie Robinson—one of the best to ever play the sport—and, to no surprise, most black and white players could not meet this standard, but this disproportionately impacted black players in subsequent years. According to Soderholm-Difatte, a social science study published in 1967 (20 years after Robinson integrated baseball) revealed that African American players had to be superior to whites to win the same position.[31]

31. Bryan Soderholm-Difatte, The Golden Era of Major League Baseball: A Time of Transition and Integration 212–13 (2015).

In 2014, I attended a diversity panel discussion featuring the Honorable Dennis Archer, one of the most accomplished attorneys of his generation. Archer, who is African American, is a former mayor of Detroit, the first African American Michigan Supreme Court justice, and the first African American president of the American Bar Association. When the discussion turned to the question and answer portion, a white lawyer in the audience prefaced his question by singing Archer's praises followed by asking where he could find the next Dennis Archer. The sentiment is nice, but the standard is unrealistic and unfair. It is the equivalent of asking a white lawyer: "Where can I find the next F. Lee Bailey?" Efforts to promote diversity and inclusion should not create standards that are unattainable by most people.

Steps taken by Rickey to integrate baseball are relevant today for law firms seeking to make sustainable, impactful, and meaningful progress in diversity and inclusion. Rickey had a clear objective grounded in fairness and business imperatives (breaking the color barrier, expanding the talent pool, and fielding the best team), he knew baseball's business and culture, and he was aware of the obstacles and that, in addition to performing at a high level, Robinson needed a champion to succeed. Rickey considered each of these factors as he set out to change the complexion of baseball. His approach is instructive to law firms. There may be certain nuances unique to your organization, but the issues are generally the same. Leaders either know the issues or they take the time to learn them and embark on methodical steps to execute in ways that move the needle. The remaining chapters in this book address various obstacles hindering law firm diversity and inclusion efforts, from educational inequality to how law firms recruit, evaluate, and promote legal talent. The chapters also draw on examples from the U.S. military and sports to provide different approaches law firms can replicate to change things.

It all comes back to leadership because change is hard and law firms often do not want to be the first to part from tradition. But as President Abraham Lincoln said, "One is a majority if he is right." This certainly proved true with Branch Rickey who integrated baseball, so now every MLB team honors Jackie Robinson's legacy by donning his iconic number 42 on April 15. The integration of the MLB illustrates several key points, and among them are the importance of knowing what obstacles impede progress, an appreciation for how long they have been in place and why, an understanding of who these obstacles intentionally and/or unintentionally benefit or disadvantage, the long-term consequences of these impediments, and the need for honesty in acknowledging the consequences in order to address these issues accordingly.

The legal profession will not reflect the diversity of the nation when a legacy of educational inequality eliminates children from contention. The next two chapters explore the origins of public education, steps taken by legislators and the judicial system to codify an educational system purposefully designed to benefit one segment of society over another, the role lawyers played to reverse this injustice, and the consequences now affecting the legal profession.

CHAPTER 3

Education: The Opportunity Gap Began as a Chasm

We seek not just freedom but opportunity. We seek not just legal equity but human ability, not just equality as a right and a theory but equality as a fact and equality as a result.

–President Lyndon B. Johnson

Introduction

The year is 2217 and the United States is patting itself on the back because the achievement gap between black and white students has finally closed. Many of you may take this statement as hyperbole but it is not. According to a report by economist Dr. Eric A. Hanushek, it will take 150–200 years to close the black-white academic achievement gap.[1] This is not attributable to the innate abilities of black and white children but has more to do with the accident of birth—the circumstances one happens to be born into. Research by the Federal Reserve Bank of St. Louis supports this. According to the study, inherited demographic characteristics such as race and parents' education level impact your economic success. And families headed by people with what the authors describe as favorable inherited demographic characteristics—being white, being over 40, and having college-educated parents—tend to be better off than families headed by people lacking those characteristics, even if

1. Eric A. Hanushek, *What Matters for Student Achievement*, Educ. Next, Spring 2016, at 19, *available at* http://educationnext.org/files/ednext_XVI_2_hanushek.pdf.

they are college educated themselves.[2] For example, $629,900 is the median net worth of middle-aged, white college graduates with a parent who also graduated from a four-year college, and $100,354 is the median net worth of a middle-aged minority college graduate whose parents did not attend college.[3] As this chapter explores in detail, skin color has determined educational worthiness throughout most of our nation's history, so many middle-aged people of color do not have college-educated parents.[4] The Federal Reserve Bank's report concludes that people are not starting on the same rung and in addition to race, the education attainment of their parents produces inherent advantages or disadvantages.

Since before the founding of our democracy, there has always been an opportunity gap resulting in an achievement gap deeply rooted along racial and socioeconomic lines. The gap begins with our youngest citizens, our children, and widens over time. Why is the achievement gap important for a book focused on diversity? It is important because future lawyers begin their training before kindergarten. In fact, the American Bar Association's Council for Racial and Ethnic Diversity in the Education Pipeline, an organization whose mission is to create a more diverse educational pipeline into the legal profession, describes prekindergarten programs as the beginning of that pipeline.[5] "The Widening Income Achievement Gap" states that the achievement gap is large when students enter kindergarten.[6] Unfortunately, this is when the weeding-out process begins. Approximately 90 percent of all American children attend public schools, and racial minorities constitute more than half of these students. A report by the Southern Education Foundation states that 51 percent of all public school children from prekindergarten through 12th

2. William R. Emmons et al., The Demographics of Wealth: 2018 Series—How Education, Race, and Birth Year Shape Financial Outcomes, Essay No. 1: The Financial Returns from College across Generations: Large but Unequal (2018).

3. White college graduates whose parents did not attend college have a median net worth of $409,110; minority college graduates with parents possessing college degrees have a median net worth of $347,586.

4. Education has also been restricted by gender, but this chapter focuses mostly on race.

5. https://www.americanbar.org/content/dam/aba/administrative/diversity_pipeline/2014_rev_ach_div_slides_1_14,_40_52_58.authcheckdam.pdf

6. Sean F. Reardon, *The Widening Income Achievement Gap*, 70 Faces Poverty 10 (2013), *available at* http://www.ascd.org/publications/educational-leadership/may13/vol70/num08/The-Widening-Income-Achievement-Gap.aspx.

grade struggle with poverty and are eligible for free or reduced-price lunches.[7] A consequence of having a majority poor public school student population is that these children start kindergarten at a disadvantage in comparison to their wealthier peers in private and public schools and may never catch up. This results in a leaky diversity pipeline where there is a disparity in academic achievement between rich, poor, minority, and nonminority children; higher dropout and expulsion rates; and lower scores on standardized tests for African American and Hispanic/Latino students. In "The Educational Pipeline to Law School—Too Broken and Too Narrow to Provide Diversity," Professor Sara Redfield of the University of New Hampshire School of Law says these factors also result in disproportionately higher levels of disengaged minority and poor children.[8] It is difficult for students facing this many obstacles to be among the pool of qualified law school applicants.

Why is it that a nation that has been in existence for more than 240 years is burdened with an opportunity gap along racial and socioeconomic lines? How did we get here and why will it take another 200 years to close the gap? Our history is filled with examples of ordinary people who faced extraordinary challenges to simply learn how to read and write because the American school system was not created equitably for everyone. A person's social status, race, gender, and religion determined if he or she was deemed worthy to be literate and thus able to fully participate in our democracy. This chapter will address the origins of educational inequality, the involvement of lawyers in perpetrating and challenging it, the lingering legacy of intentional disenfranchisement to keep masses of black and brown people undereducated, and how best to move forward in a country that will have no racial majority in a few decades.

---

7. Southern Education Foundation, A New Majority: Low Income Students Now a Majority in the Nation's Public Schools (2015), http://www.southerneducation.org/getattachment/4ac62e27-5260-47a5-9d02-14896ec3a531/A-New-Majority-2015-Update-Low-Income-Students-Now.aspx.

8. Sarah E. Redfield, *The Educational Pipeline to Law School—Too Broken and Too Narrow to Provide Diversity*, 8 Pierce L. Rev. 347 (2010), *available at* https://scholars.unh.edu/cgi/viewcontent.cgi?referer=https://www.bing.com/&httpsredir=1&article=1132&context=unh_lr.

Founding Fathers of Public Education: Thomas Jefferson and Horace Mann

Thomas Jefferson believed an educated citizenry to be critical to the survival of our fledgling democracy. According to *School: The Story of American Public Education*,[9] Jefferson believed that there should be "a crusade against ignorance" so that "every man [could] judge for himself what will secure or endanger his freedom." Public expense should be used to create a meritocracy where we "rake a few geniuses from the rubbish" so that they could attend secondary schools and universities.[10] To Jefferson, universal education served two purposes: (1) it provided the basics for participating in a democracy; and (2) it was a rehearsal for a small group of intellectual aristocrats to later serve the country. Jefferson, however, did not think everyone had the potential for genius. Girls should only receive three years of education—enough to make them good mothers and wives. And educating an African American was unfathomable.

Many of Jefferson's contemporaries found his views on educating potential farmers foolish. One such person aptly captured the views of Jefferson's detractors when he said: "Take away the food of man and his existence would cease. Take away his philosophy and he would scarcely know it was gone."[11] Jefferson would spend most of his life advocating for the creation of public schooling as secretary of state, vice president, and president, which would culminate in the creation of state-supported University of Virginia. He would establish for himself an enduring legacy that public education was essential to democracy and that "if a nation expects to be ignorant and free, it expects what never and never will be."[12] These words are also a harbinger of future government-sanctioned actions that sought to keep emancipated African Americans ignorant and quasi-enslaved.

Despite the opposition that Jefferson faced for his crusade for statewide school systems, his idea began to resonate in the 1830s and 1840s, particularly in Massachusetts through the efforts of Horace Mann. Mann was the majority

9. School: The Story of American Public Education (Sarah Mondale & Sarah B. Patton eds., 2001) (companion volume to the Public Broadcasting Service series of the same name).
10. *Id.* at 23–24.
11. *Id.* at 25.
12. *Id.*

leader of the Massachusetts state senate and would later become the secretary of education for the commonwealth—the first person in the country to hold such a title. Mann focused his attention on the quality of education students received based on their economic status. After visiting several schools across the state, Mann concluded that the system was inherently inequitable. Schools varied across Massachusetts because their support came from local taxes and fees paid by parents. Consequently, significant disparities existed in the condition of facilities; wealthy children typically stayed in school longer, and the poorest children often could not attend at all. Mann sought to rectify this by creating a system to involve the state in supervising the quality of schools. His crusade to ensure that a child's station in life not impact the quality of education did not consider how best to accommodate students of different religious beliefs. In fact, Mann believed that all schools should be rooted in (his) Protestant principles so he never considered the religious needs of students representing multiple faiths. This would present what would be seen today as an obvious problem.

The emigration of Europeans to the United States increased precipitously during the 1830s. According to the authors of *School: The Story of American Public Education*,[13] by 1840, almost half of all New York City residents were foreign born, and many of these immigrants were poor Irish Catholics who craved an education. While New York City public schools were free, they were exclusively Protestant. "Irish Catholic children were being expected to attend schools where the King James Bible was read, where Protestant hymns were being sung, where prayers were being recited, but most importantly where textbooks and the entire slant of the teaching was very much anti-Irish and very much anti-Catholic."[14]

The fight for religious equality in public education occurred simultaneously with the country's struggles with race. Before the Civil War, most African Americans lived in the South and the majority of them were enslaved and had no access to formal education. Blacks with access to an education lived in the North and attended segregated public schools in substandard conditions. In Boston, black primary school children were restricted to two schools regardless of where they lived in the city. African American parents

13. *Id.*
14. *Id.* at 33–34.

challenged this arrangement, thus beginning a more than century-long battle for educational equality.

In 1846, a group of parents presented the Boston School Committee with a petition that read in part that "the establishment of separate schools for our children deprives us of those equal privileges and advantages to which we are entitled as citizens . . . We therefore earnestly request that our children be allowed to attend schools in the Districts in which we live."[15] To assuage the parents, the school committee investigated the state of the black schools and drafted a report acknowledging deficiencies in them but took no action to desegregate or improve the schools. The African American families sued and the case, *Roberts v. City of Boston*,[16] went up to the Massachusetts Supreme Court, which sided with the City of Boston. This case is significant for at least two reasons: (1) the Massachusetts state legislature later created legislation overruling the decision; and (2) this would figure prominently 50 years later in *Plessy v. Ferguson*[17] in the formal establishment of the doctrine of "separate but equal."

Five Years of "Freedom," 95 Years of Jim Crow

In 1865—19 years after *Roberts v. City of Boston*—the Civil War ended slavery and the nation grappled with how best to educate four million people intentionally denied access to a formal education. But having spent hundreds of thousands of lives and millions of dollars to win the war, the nation would spend very little time and resources to help people transition from enslaved to citizen. This daunting task was assigned to the Freedmen's Bureau, a government program created immediately after the war for, in part, educating the masses of African Americans who craved an education to at a minimum help them get started. From 1865 to 1870, when the bureau was shut down, 4,000 schools opened across the South and nearly 250,000 people attended. Booker T. Washington described it as a "whole race trying to go to school; few were too young, and none too old, to make the attempt to learn."[18] The federal

15. *Id.* at 42.
16. Roberts v. City of Boston, 59 Mass. (5 Cush.) 198 (1850).
17. Plessy v. Ferguson, 163 U.S. 537 (1896).
18. Richard Kluger, Simple Justice: The History of *Brown v. Board of Education* and Black America's Struggle for Equality 50 (1975, 2004).

government allocated a little more than $5 million, or $1.25 per person, to help recently freed men, women, and children integrate into society. While the Freedmen's Bureau's schools encouraged southern legislatures to provide for public education programs, it would take several decades to provide even modest amounts of local or state funding for these schools.

The Birth of the Jim Crow Era and Unequal Educational Opportunities

The end of Reconstruction (and with it the end of the Freedmen's Bureau) meant that educational strides made by African Americans would become more difficult. Toward the end of the 19th century, the U.S. Supreme Court rendered a series of decisions that solidified a racial caste system that would impact public services, including education. The case that set the tone involved a law passed by the Louisiana legislature in 1890 entitled "An Act to Promote the Comfort of Passengers." The law stated that "all railway companies carrying passengers in their coaches in this State, shall provide equal but separate accommodations for the white, and colored races by providing two or more passenger coaches for each passenger train, or by dividing the passenger coaches by a partition so as to secure separate accommodations."[19]

While discriminatory practices had been common throughout the South, Louisiana, and in particular New Orleans, was different due to its fusion of black, Indian, French, and Anglo-Saxon cultures, and a very visible and vocal African American community. As a result, people did not sit quietly by when the state legislature passed the bill. They protested the legislation and said the law would "give license to the evilly-disposed . . . [to] with impunity insult, humiliate, and maltreat inoffensive persons . . . who should happen to have . . . dark skin."[20]

The African American community did more than voice its displeasure with the law; they challenged it. On June 7, 1892, Homer Adolph Plessy, an African American man described as "exceedingly light-skinned," intentionally sat in a car reserved for whites to test the law. The conductor immediately asked Plessy to move to the car for black passengers. He refused and was

19. *Id.* at 71.
20. *Id.* at 71–72.

arrested. Plessy sued, and the case eventually went to the Supreme Court as *Plessy v. Ferguson*.

As precedent, *Plessy* relied on *Roberts*, the 50-year-old Massachusetts Supreme Court case that first declared "separate but equal" educational facilities lawful. In *Plessy*, the U.S. Supreme Court determined that the issue was whether the railway segregation law was a justifiable use of the state's police power. The Court concluded that it was so long as it conformed to the "established usages, customs and traditions of the people."[21] Considering that segregation laws were new, the only applicable customs and traditions of the people were those derived from slavery. In response to concerns about the potential psychological impact of segregation laws, the Court said that segregation did not "stamp the colored race with a badge of inferiority," and if it did that was because "the colored race chooses to put the construction upon it."[22]

While the majority opinion failed to acknowledge the potential long-term consequences of its decision, the dissent was prescient:

> The present decision, it may well be apprehended, will not only stimulate aggressions, more or less brutal and irritating, upon the admitted rights of colored citizens, but will encourage the belief that it is possible, by means of state enactments, to defeat the beneficent purposes which the people of the United States had in view when they adopted the recent amendments of the Constitution . . . Sixty millions of whites are in no danger from the presence here of eight millions of blacks. The destinies of the two races, in this country, are indissolubly linked together, and the interests of both require that the common government of all shall not permit the seeds of race hate to be planted under the sanction of law.[23]

Unfortunately, the progeny of *Plessy*, beginning with a case in Georgia, would ensure this outcome. In 1899, three years after *Plessy v. Ferguson*, the Court heard its first case involving separate schools for black and white

21. *Id.* at 79.
22. *Id.*
23. *Id.* at 81.

children in *Cumming v. Richmond County Board of Education*.[24] Richmond County, Georgia, had a high school for white girls, a high school for white boys, and one high school for black boys and girls. After conducting an assessment, the county determined that there were not enough facilities to accommodate all grade school-aged black children. So the county converted the black high school into a grade school and suggested high school-aged African American children attend church-affiliated schools because this decision effectively shuttered the only black high school for the county. In siding with the Richmond County Board of Education, the Court said states were best equipped to address the maintenance of schools paid for by state taxes and federal authority had no right to interfere in the management of these schools in the absence of a "clear and unmistakable disregard" of rights provided by the U.S. Constitution.[25] The denial of a public education for black high school-aged children did not rise to that level.

Nine years after *Cumming*, the Court decided another case that gave states authority to ban all contact between the races in private and public schools. *Berea College v. Kentucky*[26] involved a small liberal arts school that had an interracial student body ever since its founding in 1859, before the Civil War. In the burgeoning years of the Jim Crow era, the state of Kentucky found the mixing of the races objectionable and passed a broad law clearly targeting Berea College that allowed institutions to teach both races at the same time provided the classes were conducted 25 miles apart! Berea College sued and lost at the state level and ultimately at the Supreme Court. The Court, again erring on the side of supporting states' rights, held the law constitutional because it did not prohibit Berea College from teaching students of each race in the same place, so long as it was at different times or at the same time but in different places. With that, *Berea College* made separate but (un)equal constitutional in all aspects of society regardless of how these laws impacted the nation's African American citizens.

Jim Crow laws flooded the South in the wake of *Plessy*, *Cumming*, and *Berea College*. These laws dictated where people lived, where people sat at sporting events, which water fountains were used by black and white people,

24. Cumming v. Richmond County Bd. of Educ., 175 U.S. 528 (1899).
25. Kluger, *supra* note 18, at 83.
26. Berea Coll. v. Kentucky, 211 U.S. 45 (1908).

and made school segregation universal—sowing the seeds of an educational opportunity gap that persists today and could continue into the 23rd century. While schools were separate, they were never equal. According to Richard Kluger in *Simple Justice: The History of* Brown v. Board of Education *and Black America's Struggle for Equality*, by 1910, there was a significant disparity in educational funding along racial lines with 11 southern states spending an average of $9.45 on white students and $2.90 on black students. And the disparity only worsened in six years because by 1916 per capita spending on white children increased to $10.32 and decreased for black children to $2.89.[27]

The law permitted this discrepancy in educational spending along racial lines and leading scholars validated it by propagating theories about the intellectual inferiority of black people. For example, in 1884, the future dean of Harvard's Lawrence Scientific School justified the disenfranchisement of the African American by citing his "animal nature."[28] In the early 1900s, other scholars wrote books peddling the intellectual shortcomings of African Americans beginning with Charles Carroll's *The Negro a Beast, or: In the Image of God*. In 1900, University of Virginia Faculty Chairman Paul B. Barringer told the Southern Education Association that African Americans should be limited to "Sunday-school training" because their skills were best suited to being a "source of cheap labor for a warm climate."[29]

Just as the beliefs of black inferiority gained momentum, the 20th century brought forth the widespread usage of intelligence tests. French psychologist Alfred Binet invented the first known assessment in 1905 to identify children in need of special education services, not to measure intelligence.[30] According to Dr. Beverly Daniel Tatum in *Can We Talk about Race? And Other Conversations in an Era of School Resegregation*, Binet believed intelligence could not be captured with a single score because it was too multidimensional. He warned against using these tests to rank and label children and stressed that they be used for the limited purpose of helping children with identifiable learning disabilities.[31]

---

27. Kluger, *supra* note 18, at 88.
28. *Id.* at 85.
29. *Id.*
30. Beverly Daniel Tatum, Can We Talk about Race? And Other Conversations in an Era of School Resegregation 42 (2007).
31. *Id.*

Leading American psychologists disregarded Binet's concerns and used these exams for exactly what Binet cautioned against: ranking and labeling children. According to Dr. Tatum, the ideas of reification and hereditarianism fueled the misuse of these tests. Reification is the assumption that test scores represent a single, measurable characteristic of brain functioning called general intelligence. And hereditarianism assumes that intelligence is mostly inherited, measurable by tests, and has no connection to independent environmental and social factors beyond a person's control (e.g., disparate treatment based on race, ethnicity, and/or gender). The hereditarian theory grew in popularity during the early 20th century due in part to Jim Crow and extreme nationalism with increased immigration of southern and eastern Europeans. Prominent psychologists Henry Herbert Goddard and Lewis M. Terman promoted the widespread usage of these tests throughout America.

Goddard brought Binet's scale to America, and Stanford University Professor Lewis Terman introduced it to American schools. Terman created a standardized test he named the Stanford-Binet Intelligence Scale, which would result in a single number called the intelligence quotient (IQ test). Terman viewed intelligence as a fixed and unchanging inherited characteristic that was in short supply for people of color irrespective of societal norms and legal factors that inhibited their ability to attain a quality education. Terman came to the following conclusion after administering the IQ test:

> Among the laboring men and servant girls there are thousands like them. They are the world's "hewers of wood and drawers of water." And yet, as far as intelligence is concerned, the tests have told the truth . . . No amount of school instruction will ever make them intelligent voters or capable citizens in the true sense of the word . . . The fact that one meets this type with such frequency among Indians, Mexicans, and Negroes suggests quite forcibily that the whole question of racial differences in the mental traits will have to be taken up anew and by experimental methods. . . . Children of this group should be segregated in special classes and be given instruction which is concrete and practical. They cannot master abstractions, but they can often be made efficient workers, able to look out for themselves. There is no possibility at the present convincing

> society that they should not be allowed to reproduce, although from a eugenic point of view they constitute a grave problem because of their unusually prolific breeding.[32]

By 1913, IQ tests indicated that twice as many blacks as whites were deemed "mentally retarded" for their ages. Reputable scientists went so far as to state that black school children were only 75 percent as capable as white students, and IQ tests of more than 100,000 World War I soldiers found that approximately 85 percent of African Americans scored lower than whites.[33] These statistics only buttressed beliefs of the mental inferiority of African Americans and gave license to politicians to espouse racist views. For example, during the 1920 presidential campaign, candidate Warren Harding said, "There is abundant evidence of the dangers which lurk in racial differences."[34] But despite these studies and rhetoric, there was a growing movement of social science that questioned and contradicted the prevailing studies of intelligence as a characteristic predetermined by race. More objective studies concluded that mental and temperamental characteristics of people had more to do with culture and environment than race. These studies would prove helpful in litigation to attain educational equality because segregation laws were justified, in part, by widely held views that investing in educating African Americans would prove futile because of their inherent intellectual inferiority.

The 19th century ended with the birth of Jim Crow and the 20th century ushered in its accelerated maturation. The law, science, social psychology, and prevailing societal attitudes about race and intelligence would make institutionalized inequality a way of life, which would profoundly impact educational opportunities and full participation in all aspects of society for African Americans. The stage was set for a small cadre of courageous and creative lawyers to use a judicial system—that often worked against them—to fight against consequences of "separate but equal."

32. *Id.* at 46.
33. KLUGER, *supra* note 18, at 306.
34. *Id.*

CHAPTER 4

From Maryland to Kansas: Legal Battles to End Segregation

"We the people"—it is a very eloquent beginning. But when the Constitution of the United States was completed on the seventeenth of September in 1787, I was not included in that "We the people." I felt for many years that somehow George Washington and Alexander Hamilton just left me out by mistake. But through the process of amendment, interpretation, and court decision, I have finally been included in "We the People."

–U.S. Congresswoman Barbara Jordan

The Command Post: Howard University

Today it is easy to look back and imagine that schools would eventually become integrated and that segregation as a lawful practice would end. But neither was guaranteed. The past century was filled with racial strife fueled by a strong desire to maintain the status quo, which intentionally kept swaths of people undereducated and unable to participate in the nation's democracy. People who challenged this risked their livelihoods and, in many instances, their lives to do so. But despite insurmountable odds and potentially dire consequences, people did fight for equality and many of these folks would be lawyers trained at a historically black institution in Washington, D.C.

Leading African American intellectuals felt a sense of urgency and concluded that black people had to lead this effort and needed a training ground from which to do so. Howard University would become that place. Founded in 1867 as part of the Freedmen's Bureau, Howard was the preeminent educational institution for African Americans. The university provided secondary school, undergraduate, graduate, and professional programs. Because graduate and professional schools in the South did not accept African Americans, Howard supplied most of the nation's black doctors, lawyers, dentists, nurses, and engineers. Despite being the place for producing a small, educated black middle class, the university suffered from the same level of neglect that plagued other institutions for African Americans and was in dire need of strong leadership. From Howard's establishment in 1867, it had been led by white men. That would change in 1926 when a 36-year-old ordained Baptist minister would become the first black president of Howard University.

Mordecai W. Johnson, described as fearless and granite-willed, was exactly what the university needed to become the sword and shield in the battle for equality. While Howard University was arguably the most prestigious black university in the nation, its only accredited programs were its medical and dental schools and it was looked down upon by African Americans educated in elite northeastern universities. Undeterred, Johnson accepted the challenge and was determined to make Howard a premiere educational institution that would create future African American leaders. Based on advice from a prominent Washington, D.C., lawyer, he saw reforming the law school as his first order of business.

In *Simple Justice: The History of* Brown v. Board of Education *and Black America's Struggle for Equality*, Richard Kluger describes Louis Brandeis, the first Jewish lawyer appointed to the U.S. Supreme Court, as having a reputation for receptivity to social experimentation and being a defender of underdogs. In a meeting with Dean Johnson, Justice Brandeis said he recognized the deficiency in the training African American lawyers received based anecdotally on reading briefs written by them. Brandeis strongly encouraged Johnson to hire a first-rate faculty to equip black law students with the skills necessary to compete in a judicial system already tilted against them.[1]

Brandeis's message resonated with Johnson who recognized the need for well-trained black lawyers. In 1926, there were 12 million African Americans

1. Richard Kluger, Simple Justice: The History of *Brown v. Board of Education* and Black America's Struggle for Equality 125 (1975, 2004).

living in America. And of that number, there were only 1,100 African American lawyers and fewer than 100 of them had been trained at reputable law schools. Johnson needed to hire a law school dean who would be the architect behind building a faculty that would produce African American lawyers with the skills necessary to shoulder the burden of the coming battle for civil rights.[2] Johnson sought a reputable, pedigreed scholar young enough to relate to his students and with the gravitas to demand respect from them. That man was Charles Hamilton Houston, a 34-year-old Harvard-trained lawyer and part-time Howard University Law School professor who spent most of his time running his law firm Houston & Houston. During his six years as the dean of Howard University Law School, Houston would turn it into a credible law school that would produce legal titans in the struggle for civil rights.

Houston, similarly to Johnson, appreciated the importance of having well-trained African American lawyers and exuded a sense of urgency. The stakes for potential African American lawyers were high and appeared to be insurmountable. Law school was different from medical school. Anatomy and physiology is the same for everyone regardless of race. While in theory the law should apply equitably to blacks and whites, it did not. So not only did Houston feel compelled to teach his students the law and its meaning, but he also wanted them to know its practical application to African Americans and equip them with the tools to eradicate the differences in application. Kluger described Howard University Law School as a laboratory for civil rights law.[3] Class sizes were intentionally small and students engaged in experiential learning that involved working on real briefs for real cases. Their education was similar to an apprenticeship because they learned at the feet of Houston and other faculty members by accompanying them to court to observe the practice of law.

The Margold Report: The Blueprint

Building a credible law school was not enough to fight against segregation. Lawsuits require money and for many years the National Association for the Advancement of Colored People (NAACP) funded these cases and did so with

2. *Id.*
3. *Id.* at 128.

the goodwill of benefactors who supported progressive causes. But resources were limited and a formidable challenge against "separate but equal" would require a steady flow of cash, a strategy, and a team of lawyers who could undertake this gargantuan task. Dean Houston would be at the center of a combination of all three.

In 1929, the NAACP received a $100,000 grant to conduct a legal campaign to enfranchise African Americans in the South. This was the first time that the NAACP had adequate resources to a devise a sustainable and strategic legal campaign to attack discrimination, and particularly the impact of "separate but equal" on the education of African American children. One outstanding issue, however, was to identify the person capable of developing and executing a strategy that would ultimately serve as the framework for the legal battle for civil rights for generations to come. Recognizing the enormity of the task, the NAACP sought advice from Dean Houston to identify someone to oversee this endeavor. Houston nominated Nathan Margold, the architect responsible for developing the blueprint that would eventually dismantle "separate but equal." Margold attended Harvard Law School with Houston and they worked on the *Harvard Law Review* together. Before Houston tapped Margold for this assignment, he served as an assistant U.S. attorney for the Southern District of New York, taught briefly at Harvard Law School, worked in private practice, and represented the Pueblo Indian tribes in land-title claims as their special counsel. Margold was considered a "brilliant man of the law."[4]

The NAACP initially recommended a series of lawsuits in states with the most flagrant difference in allocation of funds between educating black and white children. Margold considered this approach to be overly burdensome because it would require multiple suits to fight for an equal allocation of funding in several school districts, while chipping away at the NAACP's limited funds. Margold thought it more effective to attack the heart of the matter: the constitutional validity of segregation as "provided and administered."[5] Margold, keenly aware of the law and the sentiments of the day, knew that it would be futile to attempt to deprive southern states of their "acknowledged privilege

4. *Id.* at 133.
5. *Id.* at 134.

of providing separate accommodations for the two races."[6] In *Plessy v. Ferguson*,[7] the U.S. Supreme Court made racial segregation constitutional so long as the separate facilities were equal, so Margold's approach was to hold the worst offending states accountable in making sure that the "equal" in "separate but equal" actually meant "equal" in fact. He came up with a two-pronged approach to attack separate and un-equal schools: (1) end segregation laws in states that legitimized inequitable spending on educating African American children; and (2) ban segregation in states that were habitual offenders of inequality.

The Margold Report was creative, strategic, and ahead of its time, and Houston decided not to pursue Margold's strategy. Racial tensions were high, and the country was in the midst of the Great Depression. It was unlikely that there would be an appetite for litigation to spur equitable funding in educating black children. Furthermore, Houston was more focused on his more immediate and urgent responsibility of developing competent black lawyers to engage in a long-term battle against segregation.[8] However, Houston would encourage his acolytes to employ a modified version of Margold's approach by first going after graduate and professional schools. Because of segregation, there were only two graduate school programs in the South that admitted African Americans (Howard and Meharry Medical College in Nashville, Tennessee).[9] Houston believed white graduate institutions presented the best place to initiate school integration: whites were most vulnerable there since black southerners only had two graduate school options and this approach would arouse a less vitriolic reaction from whites.[10] The calculus was that the peaceful desegregation of graduate schools would trickle down to undergraduate colleges and eventually grade schools. This approach would be used by Houston's best-known student, Thurgood Marshall, who graduated from Howard University Law School in 1933 and would eventually lead the NAACP's fight in dismantling segregation one graduate program at a time.

6. *Id.*
7. Plessy v. Ferguson, 163 U.S. 537 (1896).
8. Kluger, *supra* note 1, at 136.
9. *Id.*
10. *Id.*

Separate Clearly Means Separate, but Equal Must Also Mean Equal

Murray v. Pearson,[11] the first case to successfully argue it was unlawful to have nothing approaching educational equality for African Americans, involved the University of Maryland Law School. In 1935, Marshall, then running his own practice, worked with Houston to help Donald Murray gain admission to the law school. Murray wanted to practice law in Baltimore and despite having the credentials and there being no laws segregating colleges in Maryland, Murray was denied admission. Murray sued the University of Maryland, and Houston and Marshall successfully used the Margold strategy by attacking the inequality of the system as administered since there was no law school for African Americans in the state of Maryland. In closing, Marshall argued that the U.S. Supreme Court legitimized the "separate" part of "separate but equal" in several cases, but the absence of a school for African Americans had never been tested on grounds of equality.[12] Murray won at the trial level, the Maryland Court of Appeals upheld the opinion, and the state chose not to appeal to the U.S. Supreme Court. In 1936, less than 100 years ago, Donald Murray became the first African American to attend the University of Maryland Law School and his case would provide the formula for attacking "separate but equal" in education cases at the federal level and the first test case would arise in Missouri, a Jim Crow state.

There were very few black lawyers in Missouri outside of St. Louis. In 1936, of the 45 African American attorneys in the entire state, 30 practiced in that city. And in the previous five years, the state admitted three black lawyers to its bar. The president of the St. Louis NAACP and one of the branch directors (two of the 45 black lawyers in the state) determined this was unacceptable and challenged this by launching a test case. The NAACP brought a case on behalf of Lloyd Lionel Gaines,[13] a 25-year-old graduate of Lincoln University, Missouri's state-sponsored black college, who sought admission into the University of Missouri Law School in 1936. The law school rejected Gaines's application, but gave him options: he could apply to Lincoln, which did not have a law school but could technically provide a legal education, or

11. Murray v. Pearson, 182 A. 590 (Md. 1936).
12. KLUGER, *supra* note 1, at 190.
13. Missouri *ex rel.* Gaines v. Canada, 305 U.S. 337 (1938).

attend a school out of state and the state would pay tuition charges exceeding the cost of what he would have paid at Missouri Law School.[14] Gaines refused the offer and decided to take his chances in court.

Gaines lost the case at the trial level and it took two and a half years for his case to make it to the U.S. Supreme Court. As the case wound its way through the judicial process, the Supreme Court underwent a dramatic shift. Throughout most of the early part of the 20th century, the Court played a pivotal role in solidifying Jim Crow's hold on society and in dismantling many aspects of President Franklin D. Roosevelt's New Deal during the 1930s. But in 1937, two retirements from the Court gave Roosevelt the opportunity to appoint Hugo Black, a former trial lawyer and senator from Alabama with a reputation for supporting underdogs, and Solicitor Stanley Forman Reed, a moderate Kentucky Democrat who defended many aspects of the New Deal before the Court.[15]

On November 9, 1938, when *Missouri ex rel. Gaines v. Canada* came before the Court, there were eight justices: five considered liberal-moderates, with Black and Reed among them; one moderate-conservative; and two described as "arch-conservatives." In a 5–3 decision, the Court ruled against the University of Missouri and declared:

> The admissibility of the laws separating the races in the enjoyment of privileges afforded by the State rests wholly upon the equality of the privileges which the laws give to the separated groups within the State . . . By the operation of the laws of Missouri a privilege has been created for white law students which is denied to Negroes by reason of their race.[16]

The *Murray* and *Gaines* cases proved two things: (1) Margold's recommendation to attack the "equal" in "separate but equal" was the right decision; and (2) Dean Houston's strategy to modify the approach to go after graduate schools was also correct. But both approaches had their flaws, which would be made obvious in the next series of cases beginning with *Sipuel v. Board*

14. Kluger, *supra* note 1, at 201.
15. *Id.* at 209–10.
16. *Id.* at 211–12.

of Regents,[17] a case similar to *Gaines* that involved Ada Lois Sipuel, an African American woman who sought admission to the University of Oklahoma School of Law. Again, Marshall and the NAACP followed the Margold strategy and attacked the administration of Oklahoma's segregation laws. The U.S. Supreme Court heard the case in 1948, and delivered a unanimous per curiam opinion requiring Oklahoma "to provide Ada Sipuel with a legal education 'in conformity with the equal protection clause of the 14th Amendment and provide it as soon as it does for applicants of any group.'"[18] In response, the Oklahoma Board of Regents created a makeshift law school for African Americans at the state capitol in Oklahoma City by roping off a small section for black students and assigned them three law teachers. *Sipuel* was a setback. The Court essentially said that a state had to promptly offer something, but in actuality, anything that passed as a law school. But in two subsequent cases decided on the same day in 1950, the Court would inch a little closer toward ending segregation in graduate education.

One case, *Sweatt v. Painter*,[19] involved a black mailman named Herman Marion Sweatt who wanted to attend the University of Texas Law School because, in part, it was the best law school in the state. He applied in 1946 and the law school denied him admission because of his race. When the Court of Civil Appeals heard the case a year later, the State of Texas created a temporary law school for African Americans in downtown Austin, not far from the University of Texas campus. The makeshift law school consisted of three small basement rooms, and three first-year instructors from the University of Texas Law School taught on a part-time basis. Sweatt and his lawyers decided that was not good enough and his case went to the U.S. Supreme Court.[20]

In *McLaurin v. Oklahoma State Regents for Higher Education*,[21] George W. McLaurin, an African American man with a master's degree, wanted to earn a doctorate in education from the University of Oklahoma, which rejected him. McLaurin sued, and in an attempt to comply with *Sipuel*, the Oklahoma state legislature passed a law that allowed African Americans to attend white colleges and universities so long as they were taught on a "segregated basis"

17. Sipuel v. Bd. of Regents, 332 U.S. 631 (1948).
18. Kluger, *supra* note 1, at 258.
19. Sweatt v. Painter, 339 U.S. 629 (1950).
20. Kluger, *supra* note 1, at 259.
21. McLaurin v. Okla. State Regents for Higher Educ., 339 U.S. 637 (1950).

within these institutions. So McLaurin gained admission to the doctoral program at the University of Oklahoma but had to be quarantined from the rest of the student body.[22]

In *Sweatt*, the Supreme Court determined that the issue was whether Sweatt could receive the equivalent education at the makeshift law school as he could have from the University of Texas Law School. The Court concluded that he could not based on several measurable objective factors to include the school's reputation, resources, faculty, and alumni base. By ordering the law school to admit Sweatt, it became the first time that the Supreme Court would require that a black student attend an all-white institution on the grounds that the school created for African Americans did not provide an equal educational opportunity.[23]

The Court also ruled in McLaurin's favor but on different grounds. Because he experienced segregation within the University of Oklahoma, the issue was the legality of the segregation partly because of the stigma it created. Without mentioning the word "segregation" the Court addressed the sustainability of it when it said:

> Our society grows increasingly complex, and our need for trained leaders increases correspondingly. Appellant's case represents, perhaps the epitome of that need, for he is attempting to obtain an advanced degree in education, to become, by definition, a leader and trainer of others. Those who will come under his guidance and influence must be directly affected by the education he receives. Their own education and development will necessarily suffer to extent that his training is unequal to that of his classmates. State-imposed restrictions which produce such inequalities cannot be sustained.[24]

June 5, 1950, the day the Supreme Court delivered the *Sweatt* and *McLaurin* opinions, was a big day. It was the first time the Court gave literal meaning to the word "equal" in "separate but equal." In *Sweatt*, the Court said the equality had to be real or the separation was unconstitutional. And

22. Kluger, *supra* note 1, at 265.
23. *Id.* at 280.
24. *Id.* at 282.

in *McLaurin*, the Court declared that students attending integrated schools must not be isolated from or in any other way treated differently from the general population because of their race. Both cases were major victories for educational equality, but absent a frontal assault on *Plessy*, segregation would persist and civil rights lawyers would have to fight every unequal educational facilities case one at a time. Because a case-by-case approach was untenable, it was obvious the Margold strategy—attacking the administration of "separate but equal"—had run its course and it was time to definitively attack segregation itself as unconstitutional. This was not without risks, because a loss would reinforce *Plessy*, thus rendering a major setback for African Americans and the nation.

Brown v. Board of Education: The Frontal Assault

The Margold strategy proved successful as did the decision to initially deploy it at the graduate school level, which Houston suggested. But this was only the beginning because cases brought against institutions of higher learning were the preliminary run; the target had always been the desegregation of public grade schools. This is not to diminish the *Sweatt* and *McLaurin* victories, but the NAACP intentionally pursued universities because the thought of black and white children sharing a classroom was anathema to many whites. Consequently, there was little attention or thought given to African Americans wanting to attend graduate programs in southern states because few aspired to do so. But things were changing and the first of many cases that would eventually bring about the constitutional end of segregation began in Clarendon County, South Carolina.

In the late 1940s, African American parents in Clarendon County, South Carolina, wanted better schools for their children, so they sought a remedy in federal court in *Briggs v. Elliott*.[25] Although slavery ended in 1865, Clarendon County of the 1940s is described as a place frozen in time. A small group of whites lorded over a county with a large population of poor and under-educated or uneducated blacks with little, if any, opportunity for economic advancement. The public schools were definitely separate and far from equal. White children attended brick schools with running water. To the contrary,

25. Briggs v. Elliott, 347 U.S. 497 (1954).

schools for black children were described as "dirty shacks" with outdoor toilets. These schools clearly violated *Sweatt*, but that was not enough. Marshall and the NAACP wanted *Plessy* overturned and to accomplish this they had to produce evidence showing the psychological impact of segregation on children.[26]

In preparing for *Briggs v. Elliott*, the NAACP employed Professor Kenneth B. Clark, a social psychologist (affectionately dubbed the "Doll Man") to educate them on the harmful effects of segregation on African American children. Clark and his wife conducted a series of tests with dolls to disclose how early in life black children associated success, security, beauty, and status with being white. In addition to presenting evidence at trial showing inequitable differences in the conditions of Clarendon County public school facilities based on race, the NAACP called Professor Clark to provide expert testimony on the harmful effects of segregation, prejudice, and discrimination on the psyche of black children. Despite Clark's testimony, the federal district court ruled in favor of maintaining segregation but instructed Clarendon County public schools to immediately provide equitable educational facilities for African American students.

The trial court decision came as no surprise to the NAACP. They knew they would lose *Briggs*. But their strategy involved bringing school desegregation lawsuits in various jurisdictions throughout the country to establish a record of the salient injustices wrought by segregation that would eventually be brought before the Supreme Court. Despite the loss of *Briggs*, having Clark's testimony on the record would come in handy later. According to Kluger in *Simple Justice*, on the same day the court decided *Briggs*, NAACP lawyers went to Topeka, Kansas, for a trial that would be *the* named case that would end segregation.[27]

In 1951, Oliver Brown, a quiet man who was a welder and part-time pastor, sought to enroll his child in an all-white school in Topeka. Brown, like William Reynolds, the other African American man who attempted to enroll his son in a whites-only school in 1903, was refused. In the Reynolds case, the Kansas Supreme Court cited *Plessy*, *Roberts v. City of Boston*,[28] and other

26. Kluger, *supra* note 1, at 301–02.
27. *Id.* at 369.
28. Roberts v. City of Boston, 59 Mass. (5 Cush.) 198 (1850).

cases when it ruled unanimously against Reynolds. Brown's case would be different. Other black parents joined him, the NAACP represented them, and these lawyers established a pattern of the pernicious effects of segregation supported by credible social psychology that would later be considered on appeal by the U.S. Supreme Court.

The U.S. District Court for Kansas heard the case in June 1951. In addition to calling witnesses who testified to discrepancies of facilities for black and white school children, the NAACP lawyers called several social psychologists as expert witnesses who buttressed Clark's testimony in *Briggs*. Professor Horace B. English of the Ohio State University testified that there is no correlation between a person's race and his or her ability to learn, but if people are perpetually told—implicitly or explicitly—that they are incapable (or unworthy) of learning then they will live up to that low expectation of them. Professor English went further to say that "legal separation definitely depresses the Negro's expectancy and is therefore prejudicial to his learning."[29]

Another expert stated that segregation sent the message to black children that they were "subordinate" and "inferior" to white children. But the testimony that would potentially influence the Supreme Court came from a Kansas University professor of social psychology, Louisa Holt, who said that state-sanctioned segregation "is inevitably interpreted both by white people and by Negroes as denoting the inferiority of the Negro . . . Were it not for the sense that one group is inferior to the other, there would be no basis . . . for such segregation."[30]

In ruling against Brown and the other parents, the district court gave them a gift for appeal in the form of "findings of fact" that echoed the testimony of Holt:

> Segregation of white and colored children in public schools has a detrimental effect upon the colored children. The impact is greater when it has the sanction of law; for the policy of separating the races is usually interpreted as denoting the inferiority of the Negro group. A sense of inferiority affects the motivation of a child to learn. Segregation with the sanction of law,

29. Kluger, *supra* note 1, at 416.
30. *Id.* at 416–17.

> therefore, has a tendency to retard the educational and mental development of Negro children and to deprive them of some of the benefits they would receive in a racially integrated school.[31]

Brown v. Board of Education[32] and four other segregation cases went before the U.S. Supreme Court for the first time in the spring of 1953. The Court sought additional information from the litigants and drafted a series of questions to be answered in new briefs and during oral argument on October 1953.[33] The Court delivered its opinion in May 1954. Chief Justice Earl Warren addressed the applicability of *Plessy* directly when he defined the issue as whether "segregation of children in public schools solely on the basis of race . . . deprive the children of the minority group of educational opportunities." In concluding that it did, Chief Justice Warren cited almost verbatim the findings of fact from the Kansas District Court that relied heavily on Professor Holt's testimony.[34] The Court also rejected the language in *Plessy* that downplayed and ignored the detrimental effects of segregation when it said:

> Whatever may have been the extent of psychological knowledge at the time of *Plessy v. Ferguson*, this finding [by the Kansas court in *Brown* that segregation denotes inferiority and diminishes learning motivation] is amply supported by modern authority. Any language in *Plessy v. Ferguson* contrary to this finding is rejected.[35]

Conclusion: After *Brown v. Board of Education*

The unanimous *Brown v. Board of Education* decision by the U.S. Supreme Court overturned *Plessy* and officially ended state-sanctioned segregation. Far more broadly, in addition to education, the decision integrated all aspects of society. And, recognizing that the immediate implementation would be difficult in the South, Chief Justice Warren gave the region an opportunity to phase out segregation despite (or perhaps in spite of) court-mandated

31. *Id.* at 425.
32. Brown v. Bd. of Educ., 347 U.S. 483 (1954).
33. KLUGER, *supra* note 1, at 619.
34. *Id.* at 707–08.
35. *Id.* at 708.

integration. But many southern states resisted, resulting in the passage of several civil rights laws to ensure compliance with *Brown*. Federal agencies used these laws to spur rapid progress. For example, according to a *ProPublica* article, in 1963, 1 percent of southern African American children attended school with white children, and by the 1970s that number mushroomed to 90 percent.[36] According to Richard Rothstein of the Economic Policy Institute, many of the gains made post-*Brown* have stalled and black children are more racially and socioeconomically isolated today than in any time since the 1970s because homogenous neighborhoods lead to homogenous schools.[37]

Research conducted by Professors Raj Chetty and Nathaniel Hendren[38] concluded that the neighborhoods in which children grow up influence the probability of whether they attend college and their long-term economic mobility. Chetty and Hendren analyzed de-identified tax records from 1996 to 2012 of more than five million families who moved between different cities. As an example, the researches tracked families who moved from Cincinnati to Pittsburgh. Children born into low-income families in Cincinnati will earn on average $23,000 of income at age 26 as compared to $28,000 for someone born and raised in Pittsburgh. According to the research, a nine-year-old who moves from Cincinnati to Pittsburgh will make up 50 percent of the income difference of a child who spent his or her entire life in Pittsburgh, resulting in an approximate income of $25,500 as an adult. What they describe as the "childhood exposure effect" illustrates that a child improves the socioeconomic outcomes every extra year he or she spends in a better environment when measured against children already living in the environment.[39]

Chetty and Hendren validated the exposure effect by assessing the following: siblings within the same family who lived in better environments for different durations; families who relocated to better environments due to

---

36. Nikole Hannah-Jones, *Lack of Order: The Erosion of a Once-Great Force for Integration*, ProPublica, May 1, 2014, https://www.propublica.org/article/lack-of-order-the-erosion-of-a-once-great-force-for-integration.

37. Richard Rothstein, Economic Policy Institute, Brown v. Board at 60: Why Have We Been So Disappointed? What Have We Learned? (2014), https://www.epi.org/publication/brown-at-60-why-have-we-been-so-disappointed-what-have-we-learned/.

38. Raj Chetty & Nathaniel Hendren, The Impacts of Neighborhoods on Intergenerational Mobility: Childhood Exposure Effects and County-Level Estimates (2015), http://www.equality-of-opportunity.org/assets/documents/nbhds_exec_summary.pdf.

39. *Id.*

circumstances beyond their control, such as natural disasters; and, finally, for a more precise focus, the differences in the exposure effect across subgroups (e.g., the disparate outcomes for boys and girls living in high-crime areas). In each of the scenarios, children with longer exposure to better surroundings had superior outcomes.[40] Specifically, one sibling outperformed another, outcomes for children from involuntarily displaced families improved, and families with sons and daughters experienced better outcomes for their daughters than for their sons in areas with high crime rates.[41] Why are some areas better for upward social mobility than others? Chetty and Hendren identify five characteristics: less racial and socioeconomic segregation, lower levels of income inequality, lower violent crime rates, more two-parent households, and better schools.[42]

Their research also revealed that a child's probability of attending college increases when the child moves to a neighborhood with higher college attendance rates. A *New York Times* article by Ozan Jaquette and Karina Salazar demonstrates how neighborhood affluence or the lack thereof determines a child's exposure to the college recruiting process.[43] According to Jaquette and Salazar, approximately one-third of American household incomes exceed $100,000, but private colleges and universities conduct nearly half of their high school visits in neighborhoods with higher average incomes.[44] And public universities tend to recruit almost exclusively at affluent, predominately white out-of-state high schools where parents have the means to pay almost double or triple the tuition of in-state residents.[45] A consequence of this strategy is that students with similar levels of academic achievement from less affluent neighborhoods with greater racial and socioeconomic diversity get overlooked. This approach runs contrary to President Lyndon B. Johnson's call to action to create a better America that is not defined by one's station in life.

President Johnson knew more work remained after *Brown* and he did not mince words during his "To Fulfill These Rights" speech at Howard University's 1965 commencement. President Johnson beckoned common sense and fairness

40. *Id.*
41. *Id.*
42. *Id.*
43. Ozan Jaquette & Karina Salazar, *Colleges Recruit at Richer, Whiter High Schools*, N.Y. Times, Apr. 13, 2018, https://www.nytimes.com/interactive/2018/04/13/opinion/college-recruitment-rich-white.html.
44. *Id.*
45. *Id.*

to adequately address the legacy of systemic racial injustice that restrained ability, capped potential, and limited equitable access to opportunity:

> You do not take a person who, for years, has been hobbled by chains and liberate him, bring him up to the starting line of a race and then say, "you are free to compete with all the others," and still justly believe that you have been completely fair. Thus it is not enough just to open the gates of opportunity. All our citizens must have the ability to walk through those gates. This is the next and the more profound stage of the battle for civil rights. We seek not just freedom but opportunity. We seek not just legal equity but human ability, not just equality as a right and a theory but equality as a fact and equality as a result. . . . To this end equal opportunity is essential, but not enough, not enough. Men and women of all races are born with the same range of abilities. But ability is not just the product of birth. Ability is stretched or stunted by the family that you live with, and the neighborhood you live in—by the school you go to and the poverty or the richness of your surroundings. It is the product of a hundred unseen forces playing upon the little infant, the child, and finally the man. . . .[46]

Lawyers dedicated most of the 20th century to using the judicial system to bestow legal equity to every American in word and in deed. The blueprint that was conceived at Howard University School of Law ultimately birthed a movement that toppled segregation and forced the nation to live up to its founding ideals. More work remained, so Congress passed legislation to provide and protect civil rights and presidents signed executive orders requiring that public and private entities doing business with the government take affirmative action to provide unfettered access for people to pursue economic opportunity. Lawyers used and continue to use the law to attack institutional barriers, but self-imposed obstacles to progress remain. Chapter 5 explores how self-imposed constraints in the law school admissions process represent another choke point in the legal profession's diversity pipeline.

46. Lyndon B. Johnson, Commencement Address at Howard University: "To Fulfill These Rights," 2 Pub. Papers 635–40 (1966).

CHAPTER 5

Barriers to Entry: Limiting Merit Limits Opportunity

Since I have difficulty defining merit and what merit alone means—and in any context, whether it's judicial or otherwise—I accept that different experiences in and of itself, bring merit to the system.

–U.S. Supreme Court Justice Sonia Sotomayor

Introduction

At the 1964 Howard University commencement, President Lyndon B. Johnson declared unfair the notion that a level playing field existed in our country because the U.S. Supreme Court declared "separate but equal" unconstitutional in 1954 after centuries of institutional racism and inequity. In the speech known as the intellectual framework for affirmative action, President Johnson said legal equity alone was not enough; the next phase in the civil rights battle would be the creation of a just society affording every American unfettered access to pursue opportunity.[1] Lawyers—Charles Hamilton Houston, Nathan Margold, Thurgood Marshall, and so many others—propelled the nation toward legal equity but there were few lawyers to whom they could pass the baton. In 1965, when Johnson signed Executive Order No. 11,246 mandating affirmative steps to create economic opportunities previously denied people of color, African Americans represented 5 percent of undergraduate students

1. Lyndon B. Johnson, Commencement Address at Howard University: "To Fulfill These Rights," 2 Pub. Papers 635–40 (1966).

and 1 percent of law students.[2] Affirmative action sought to remedy these disparities in employment and education.

After decades of affirmative action programs, the results have been mixed. In 2017, analysis by the *New York Times* of 100 public flagship universities and Ivy League institutions found that despite decades of affirmative action programs, black and Hispanic students are more underrepresented today at the nation's top colleges and universities than they were in 1980.[3] Education experts attribute this to equity issues beginning with the quality of the education students receive in elementary and secondary schools, access to advanced courses, high-quality instructional materials, and adequate facilities.[4] This persistent underrepresentation impacts the demographic composition of the nation's law schools and ultimately the legal profession, which remains one of the most homogenous professions.[5] Made apparent during the early years in the fight for legal equity, a diverse legal profession is necessary for a heterogeneous country. But the vocation that fought for diversity by ensuring the fair application of constitutional rights to every American has a diversity problem.

The Law School Admissions Test

The Law School Admissions Test (LSAT) as currently used hinders the promotion of diversity in the legal profession. Professor Aaron Taylor of Saint Louis University School of Law and other prominent scholars who research this issue describe the LSAT as a "narrow test, designed only to predict first-year grades."[6] And, even in this context according to Taylor, the predictive value of the test is overstated. For example, in 2010, the median correlation

2. *Affirmative Action—Overview*, Nat'l Conf. St. Legislatures, Feb. 7, 2014, http://www.ncsl.org/research/education/affirmative-action-overview.aspx.

3. Jeremy Ashkenas et al., *Even with Affirmative Action, Blacks and Hispanics Are More Underrepresented at Top Colleges Than 35 Years Ago*, N.Y. Times, Aug. 24, 2017.

4. *Id.*

5. American Bar Association, ABA National Lawyer Population Survey: 10-Year Trend in Lawyer Demographics (2017), https://www.americanbar.org/content/dam/aba/administrative/market_research/national-lawyer-population-10-year-demographics-revised.authcheckdam.pdf.

6. Aaron N. Taylor, Reimagining Merit as Achievement (2013), https://works.bepress.com/aaron_taylor/2/.

between LSAT scores and first-year law school grades was 0.36, a low to moderate relationship. The correlation increases to 0.48 when combined with undergraduate grade point averages (UGPAs). Taylor's research reveals a weakening of the correlations when LSAT scores and UGPAs are measured against post-first-year grades and bar passage.[7] Despite, at best, a limited correlation to success as a law student and, at worst, no connection to becoming an effective lawyer, the LSAT profoundly impacts the diversity of law school students, law school rankings, financial aid decisions, law school admissions practices and strategies, and future employment opportunities. How did an exam with a tenuous correlation to succeeding as a lawyer come to have this much influence?

The legal profession began as an apprenticeship that did not require a formal legal education. Aspiring lawyers learned the practice at the feet of a seasoned attorney. At the end of the 19th century, only 20 percent of practicing attorneys possessed legal degrees.[8] In the 1900s, the American Bar Association (ABA) professionalized legal practice by making state bar membership contingent on obtaining a formal legal education.[9] This resulted in law schools developing a standardized way to evaluate law school applicants. Prior to the LSAT, law schools set their own standards for admissions decisions, but this practice changed in the 1940s.

On November 10, 1947, law school deans from Harvard, Cornell, New York University, Rutgers, Stanford, Syracuse, the University of Pennsylvania, and Yale met to discuss the creation of a standardized test to use as a supplement for law school admissions decisions. The conclusion of World War II resulted in an uptick of veterans and other nontraditional students wanting a legal degree, and law schools needed a more efficient and consistent way to screen them.[10] Prior to the LSAT, law schools used their own systems that considered the reputation of the applicant's undergraduate school and UGPA. The LSAT founders made a conscious decision to develop a test that could be a good predictor of first-year grades under the (now proven to be erroneous)

7. *Id.* at 46.

8. Aaron N. Taylor, *Robin Hood, in Reverse: How Law School Scholarships Compound Inequality*, 47 J.L. & Educ. 10 (2018).

9. *Id.*

10. William P. LaPiana, A History of the Law School Admission Council and the LSAT, Keynote Address at the 1998 Law School Admission Council Annual Meeting (May 28, 1998).

assumption that first-year grades could predict law school and legal professional success. According to New York Law School Professor William L. LaPiana, the founders considered including questions to assess "general background," which accounted for the variances of the preparatory educational training of law school applicants.[11] Ultimately, the founders rejected it, which is unfortunate because it could have been an initial effort to promote diversity in the bar.

The introduction of the LSAT proved successful for the profession; law schools finally had a uniform approach to assessing law school candidates. But contrary to the desires of the LSAT founders, the test would evolve to assume greater significance than originally intended. By the 1970s, the LSAT became the primary criterion for admissions decisions and, today, law school rankings and reputation are based largely on the test scores of first-year classes.[12] Meanwhile, overreliance on an exam with very little if any correlation to overall law school success, bar passage, and a successful legal career profoundly impacts the legal profession's stated goal of having a bar that represents the diversity of our nation. Research by Professor Taylor[13] reveals the disproportionate impact of the LSAT along race and socioeconomic status.

The highest an applicant can score on the LSAT is 180. At 142, the average score for black LSAT-takers is 11 points lower than the average for white and Asian test-takers at 153, and four points lower that Latino/Hispanic test-takers (146). Taylor analyzed data from the 2016 Law School Survey of Student Engagement (LSSSE) to provide insight into LSAT score differences based on socioeconomic background. The lowest average LSAT score of 152 came from respondents whose parents had no more than a high school diploma, whereas respondents who had at least one parent with a bachelor's degree had an average score of 155.[14] Taylor believes these figures understate socioeconomic score differences because the LSSSE pool includes only people who gained admission to and enrolled in law school.

The conclusion to draw from these statistics is obvious: better educational training occurring long before people take the LSAT and resources to prepare

11. *Id.*
12. *Id.* at 10.
13. Taylor, *supra* note 8.
14. *Id.*

for it provide advantages that inhibit diversity. The result is that in 2015, black LSAT test-takers had an average score lower than the entering class median of all but two of the approximately 200 ABA-accredited law schools.[15] And for Hispanic/Latino test-takers, only 15 schools had median scores at or below the average for this group. These test scores result in stark admission rate disparities along racial and ethnic differences. In 2014, for example, the admit rate for white applicants was 85 percent, 76 percent for Asian applicants, 71 percent for Hispanic/Latino applicants, and 56 percent for black applicants. In addition to influencing law school demographics, LSAT scores also impact financial aid decisions and determine scholarship packages.

As law schools face increasing pressure to attract the "best" students (based mostly on LSAT scores), they respond by using scholarships to entice students to attend their schools.[16] For example, from 2005 to 2010, merit scholarship funding increased by 68 percent and 53 percent among public and private law schools, respectively; need-based scholarships remained flat during the same period; and scholarships for people exhibiting financial need and merit—"need-plus" scholarships—have increased 68 percent and 59 percent at public and private law schools, respectively. According to Professor Taylor's research, "need-plus" scholarships operate as merit scholarships by another name and have little equitable impact.[17]

Many law schools depend heavily on tuition to generate revenue. For example, in 2013, tuition payments totaled an average of 69 percent of law school revenue. Approximately 50 law schools (25 percent of all schools) received at least 88 percent of their revenue from tuition.[18] This financial structure is noteworthy because students with the highest LSAT scores receive tuition discounts funded largely by tuition paid by students who least can afford to attend law school. According to Taylor, the LSAT-driven approach to awarding scholarships ensures that students from privileged backgrounds receive financial aid, while disadvantaged students pay higher tuition rates to cover the discounts provided to their wealthier peers. Taylor refers to this dynamic as the "Reverse Robin Hood" strategy, which ultimately results

15. *Id.* at 13.
16. *Id.* at 14.
17. *Id.* at 14–15.
18. *Id.*

in students with the least financial means carrying a higher student debt burden.[19]

Despite the LSAT's diversity impact, students of color are attending law school. In fact, law schools are probably more diverse than ever (in terms of percentages rather than head count). This shift is partly attributable to lower-tiered law schools (i.e., schools with the lowest median LSAT scores for incoming students) accepting disproportionately more African American and/or Hispanic students as well as the fact that fewer students are now going to law school in general. According to "Diversity as a Law School Survival Strategy" by Professor Taylor, law school student enrollment fell by 25 percent between 2010 (with a record high of 52,488 first-year students) and 2013 (with a record low of 39,675 first-year students).[20] After analyzing LSAT scores and enrollment statistics for those two years, Professor Taylor noted that schools with the highest median LSAT scores became less diverse, while the less prestigious schools became more diverse.[21]

Professor Taylor attributes this stratification to many factors, including the need for lower-tiered schools to maintain revenue by using diversity to help accomplish this goal, as well as elite law schools using the economic downturn as an opportunity to focus more on admitting students with the highest LSAT scores. This racial and ethnic stratification among law schools could have long-term consequences on the career paths and trajectories of minority students. For example, research by the Law and Society Association reveals that more than 50 percent of graduates from the top ten law schools either work in law firms with at least 250 lawyers or in prestigious federal government positions such as judicial clerkships or the Justice Department.[22] On the contrary, only 4 percent of graduates of lower tiered schools work in law firms with more than 250 lawyers, and many of these graduates work in small, solo practices or in state government jobs.[23]

---

19. *Id.* at 15.

20. Aaron N. Taylor, *Diversity as a Law School Survival Strategy*, 59 St. Louis U. L.J. 321 (2015), *available at* http://goo.gl/wQYpru.

21. *Id.* at 348–49.

22. Ronit Dinovitzer & Bryant G. Garth, *Lawyer Satisfaction in the Process of Structuring Legal Careers*, 41 Law & Soc'y Rev. 11 (2007).

23. *Id.*

Dramatic increases in the enrollment of African American and Hispanic law students must occur to combat the stratification Professor Taylor warns against. In "The Educational Pipeline to Law School—Too Broken and Too Narrow to Provide Diversity," Professor Sara Redfield of the University of New Hampshire School of Law states that by 2030, the overall lawyer population will be an estimated 1.1 million, and drastic changes would have to occur for African American and Hispanic attorneys to approach parity with their representation in the general population.[24] Specifically, the profession would have to add 100,000 and 230,000 black and Hispanic lawyers, respectively. That would require increasing current African American admission rates by 45 percent, from currently 3,980 per year to approximately 5,800, and increasing Hispanic admission rates by a staggering 195 percent, from currently 4,400 per year to approximately 13,000 per year.[25] Based on previous and current law school enrollment statistics, it is highly unlikely that increases of this magnitude will occur. But what if law schools took a different approach to merit as a way to promote diversity in their admissions practices? Professor Taylor of Saint Louis University School of Law proposes such an approach.

Reconsidering What Constitutes Merit in the Law School Admissions Process

In "Reimagining Merit as Achievement," Taylor calls for the use of the Achievement Framework to consider context when evaluating achievement and merit in the law school admissions process.[26] Merriam-Webster Dictionary defines "merit" as "a character or conduct deserving reward, honor, or esteem."[27] But the character and conduct worthy of esteem are based on subjective factors created by those who have benefited most from how merit has traditionally been defined and applied. The result is a meritocracy that is a limited indicator of ability and rewards people with access to resources that can give them

---

24. Sarah E. Redfield, *The Educational Pipeline to Law School—Too Broken and Too Narrow to Provide Diversity*, 8 PIERCE L. REV. 347 (2010), *available at* http://scholars.unh.edu/unh_lr/vol8/iss3/5.

25. *Id.* at 350.

26. TAYLOR, *supra* note 6.

27. Merriam-Webster Dictionary, *Merit*, https://www.merriam-webster.com/dictionary/merit (last visited July 31, 2018).

a competitive advantage. The Achievement Framework acknowledges that people do not have equal access to opportunity and that intentional actions are required to level the playing field. In addition to considering where people end up, this broad approach to merit also considers what people overcome to succeed.

The Achievement Framework is grounded in the "merit-aware model" created by the late Dr. William F. Goggin, who sought to create a fair, just, and accurate admissions process that considered actual merit and not just absolute test scores. Dr. Goggin once said, "Does anyone, anywhere believe that a student's absolute test score is a perfect measure of anything, much less merit?"[28] He challenged institutions of higher education with a sincere commitment to diversity to create an admissions process that "measure[s] the extent to which a student's achievement exceed[s] what could have reasonably been expected given . . . her academic background."[29]

In "Merit-Aware Admissions in Public Universities," researchers identify the following as the two biggest challenges to promoting diversity in selective universities: having a critical mass of qualified minority applicants and using a screening process that considers merit in a fair and just way resulting in a diverse screened-applicant pool.[30] Professor Taylor's Achievement Framework advocates for the creation of a law school admissions process that converts life's disadvantages into advantages as a way to take a more holistic approach to defining merit. It is a deliberate attempt to create a fairer process for applicants who may have lacked the resources to attend the best schools, but still achieved beyond what could have reasonably been expected of them under their circumstances. The framework acknowledges that not all talented students have access to the best training, and intentional measures must be taken to ensure that they are not barred from opportunities because they are competing in a tournament against students who have been in training most of their educational lives.

The framework tackles class-consciousness while providing a race-neutral way to promote racial and ethnic diversity. This is significant because,

---

28. Edward P. St. John et al., *Merit-Aware Admissions in Public Universities*, NEA Higher Educ. J. 37 (2000).

29. *Id.*

30. *Id.*

according to Professor Taylor, approaches focused solely on socioeconomic diversity have hurt racial diversity because they disproportionately assist poor whites due to their overrepresentation in the general population. For example, University of California, Los Angeles, Law School experienced a 70 percent drop in the representation of black first-year law students after instituting a class-conscious affirmative action program.[31] Unlike socioeconomic affirmative action programs, the Achievement Framework includes factors that address race-based and educational disparities.

The law school admissions process is among the most selective in higher education. For example, in 2011, 154 of the 201 ABA-accredited law schools had admission rates below 50 percent.[32] Legal scholars have described selective admissions processes as "the preserve of the advantaged" or "social engineering to preserve the elite."[33] Embedded preferences in selective admissions favor people with means. And the Achievement Framework is designed to ensure that people of lesser means—particularly those from underrepresented racial and ethnic groups—are no longer disadvantaged in selective admissions processes, such as those that law schools use.

The law school admissions criteria vary among schools but they all consider LSAT scores, UGPAs, and personal statements. Some law schools determine an applicant's relative strength through an index-based process that applies LSAT scores and UGPAs to a numerical formula. The formulas are designed to predict certain outcomes (e.g., a higher index value may predict higher first-year grades). Law schools using the index create classifications that determine the treatment applicants receive in the admissions process and the likelihood of admission:[34]

- High index value (presumptive admit)
- Middling index value (committee review)
- Low index value (presumptive deny)

Law schools perform a cursory review of the presumptive admits and of the presumptive denies mostly to verify the original presumption;

31. Taylor, *supra* note 6, at 6–7.
32. *Id.* at 53.
33. *Id.* at 52.
34. *Id.* at 53–54.

consequently, applicants falling into these two categories are usually offered or denied admission. Final decisions are most difficult to predict for applicants in the middling index value (committee review) because they receive the fullest consideration. Taylor's Achievement Framework is modeled after an index-based admissions process with two classifications: the Overachievement Index and the Disadvantage Index.

Overachievement Index

The Overachievement Index measures an applicant with a high LSAT/UGPA index value against what is reasonable to expect based on his or her circumstances. It weighs the applicant's LSAT/UGPA against two factors: (1) the median LSAT/UGPA index value of the law school's prior-year entering class; and (2) the median LSAT/UGPA index value of other law school applicants from the same undergraduate school. Use of the median LSAT/UGPA index value of the immediate prior entering class as a benchmark contextualizes merit in comparison to the most recent group of students admitted to a particular law school. Consideration of the median LSAT/UGPA of an applicant's undergraduate peers puts the applicant's background into context. According to Professor Taylor, the choice of an undergraduate institution reflects financial, social, academic, and personal factors resulting in a "routing effect" that creates homogeneities within institutions. A consequence is that wealthy and poorer students attend different schools. Evaluating an applicant's index value against his or her peers is a more robust and equitable way to assess the applicant's achievement level. This benchmark could make black and Hispanic applicants more competitive because lower median LSAT scores disadvantage them in the admissions process.

How the Overachievement Index Works

An "Overachiever" is an applicant whose value exceeds either benchmark. A "High Overachiever" is an applicant whose value exceeds either benchmark by a preset amount (or more).[35] The significance of these classifications will be explained later. Only the exceeding value will be considered for classification purposes if one value exceeds one benchmark, but not the other.[36]

35. *Id.* at 54.
36. *Id.*

Disadvantage Index

The Disadvantage Index measures socioeconomic and education disadvantages overcome by the applicant. The index comprises six factors:[37]

- **Applicant's net worth** (if under age 30, parents' net worth). Net worth is positively associated with college-going and educational attainment rates. In calculating net worth, schools would require applicants to provide an accounting of all assets (e.g., real estate, automobiles, stocks and bonds, jewelry, cash) and all liabilities (e.g., mortgages, student loans, credit card debts). Applicants of lower net worth would benefit most from inclusion of this factor in the index.
- **Applicant's income** (if under age 30, parents' income). Income is positively associated with college-going and educational attainment rates. Applicants with lower income would benefit most from inclusion of this factor in the index.
- **Applicant's first-generation college student status**. First-generation college status is negatively associated with college attendance and completion. Applicants who are first-generation college students would benefit most from inclusion of this factor in the index.
- **Applicant's Pell Grant status**. Pell Grants are federal education grants for undergraduate students with unmet financial need. Lower socioeconomic status is negatively associated with college completion. Applicants who received Pell Grants in college would benefit most from inclusion of this factor in the index.
- **Percentage of Pell-eligible students at applicant's undergraduate college or university**. An institution's percentage of Pell-eligible students is a reflection of the socioeconomic status of its students. Selective, well-endowed institutions tend to enroll fewer Pell-eligible students than less selective and less well-funded institutions. Applicants who attended institutions that enrolled high percentages of Pell-eligible students would benefit most from inclusion of this factor in the index.

37. *Id.* at 56–57.

- **Graduation rate of applicant's undergraduate college or university.** Colleges and universities with lower graduation rates send proportionally fewer students to graduate and professional school than institutions with higher graduation rates. These schools tend to have fewer resources, serving students of lower socioeconomic status and offering fewer safety nets for those who encounter academic or financial problems. A student who graduates from such an institution has likely had to work harder and overcome more obstacles, with less institutional assistance, than the typical graduate of a school with a higher graduation rate. Applicants who attended undergraduate schools with lower graduation rates would benefit most from inclusion of this factor in the index.

Each factor in the Disadvantage Index is assigned a numerical value. For example, there could be binary factors for first-generation status assigned values based on the two possible outcomes, or there could be continuum-based factors for income using national data or intra-applicant comparisons to provide contextual information. To avoid the blunt impact of class-conscious affirmative action programs and to promote racial and ethnic diversity, Professor Taylor suggests using nuanced assessments of wealth percentiles to account for the grinding poverty disproportionately affecting black and Hispanic people.[38]

How the Disadvantage Index Works

Law schools would measure the resulting Disadvantage Index value against a median Disadvantage Index value of its previous entering class. A "Disadvantaged" applicant is someone who overcame more disadvantages than the benchmark. A "Highly Disadvantaged" applicant is someone from a particularly acute level of disadvantage.

Professor Taylor uses the following example to illustrate how law schools could consider disadvantage: John Smith, an applicant to Rich Law School, has a Disadvantage Index value of 21. The median value for Rich Law's previous entering class was 13. Rich Law uses a formula that assigns higher values

38. *Id.* at 58.

to higher levels of disadvantage; thus, John would be deemed "Disadvantaged" if Rich Law decided to confer that status on any applicant whose value exceeded the previous year's median by, say, five or more points.[39]

The Relationship between the Overachievement and Disadvantage Indexes

The Overachievement and Disadvantage Indexes both contain three classifications. For the Overachievement Index, applicants are classified as Overachievers, High Overachievers, or No Overachievement. The Disadvantage Index includes the following classifications: Disadvantaged, Highly Disadvantaged, or Not Disadvantaged. Law schools could base admissions decisions on an applicant's classification on each index. Table 1 below illustrates how this would work.

Table 1: Reimagining Merit as Achievement[40]

	No Overachievement	Overachiever	High Overachiever
Not Disadvantaged	Presumptive Deny	Committee Review	Presumptive Admit
Disadvantaged	Committee Review	Presumptive Admit	Presumptive Admit
Highly Disadvantaged	Presumptive Admit	Presumptive Admit	Presumptive Admit

As illustrated in the table, the Achievement Framework prefers and rewards overachievement and disadvantage. "High Overachiever" and "Highly Disadvantaged" applicants are considered presumptive admits. Applicants whose LSAT/UGPA index values exceed either of the two benchmarks set by the law school will likely gain admission regardless of their disadvantage level. And, under Professor Taylor's approach, "Highly Disadvantaged" applicants are presumptive admits regardless of their level of overachievement.

Law schools will presumptively deny applicants suffering no disadvantage and lacking overachievement even if their LSAT scores and UGPAs appear to

39. *Id.*
40. *Id.* at 59.

be acceptable. The two factors provide context lacking from a review process that overemphasizes performance on a standardized test as if all applicants are afforded the same opportunities to score well. The modified admissions process will view applicants' qualifications through the lens of social inequality that could promote racial and ethnic diversity in selective higher education institutions.

Research supports Professor Taylor's framework. Goggin, on whose model the framework is based, advocated rewarding students who exceed reasonable expectations in the admissions process as a response to increased opposition to race-conscious affirmative action programs. He believed a more expansive view of merit considering circumstances beyond an applicant's control could be an effective way to promote racial diversity. Below are two examples taken from research published by the *NEA Higher Education Journal* on how a merit-aware approach can promote diversity in two public undergraduate institutions with varying degrees of diverse representation by using the following three-step process to create a merit index:[41]

- Calculate the average Scholastic Assessment Test (SAT) score for each high school by using all students' scores from a given high school for those students attending public colleges or universities in the state the prior academic year.
- Calculate a merit index for all students based solely on positive merit scores (e.g., subtracting the average SAT score of an applicant's high school from the applicant's score).
- Weight merit to recognize high-achieving students from high schools with lower than average achievement test scores. Students from the lowest achieving schools received the highest weights. This approach acknowledges that the admissions process playing field is not level for students attending lesser-quality schools.

The index based exclusively on merit increased significantly the diversity in the screened-applicant pool for both institutions and had a positive association with first-year persistence. Tables 2 and 3 demonstrate the impact

41. St. John et al., *supra* note 28, at 39–40.

of the merit index on the applicant pools of two college campuses. One campus is located in a homogenous part of the state and attracts few minority candidates. The other campus is more diverse and has a history of attracting large percentages of minority candidates. In both cases, researchers screened 30 percent of the applicants using an SAT cutoff score of 1160, and then screened another 10 percent and used the weighted merit index to select the top students.

Table 2: Application of the Merit-Aware Approach in Selective University—Traditional Campus[42]

Ethnic Group	Applicant Pool (%)	Percent w/ SAT ≥ 1160 (A)	Percent in Merit Group (B)	Percent in Screened Pool (A+B)
American Indian	0.3	0.1	0.5	0.2
Asian	2.7	4.4	2.6	3.9
Black	3.2	1.1	6.1	2.5
Foreign National	0.1	0.2	0.1	0.2
Hispanic	1.8	1.2	1.7	1.3
Other American	1.0	0.8	0.9	0.8
White	90.1	90.3	87.7	89.6
Not specified	0.9	1.9	0.4	1.5

In Table 2, the merit index increased overall diversity by approximately 3 percent, while the SAT index decreased diversity by 0.2 percent. The application of the merit index more than doubled the percentage of black students in the screened-applicant pool. Blacks constituted 3.2 percent of the applicant population, 1.1 percent of the initial group with the SAT cutoff of 1160, and 6.1 percent of the merit group. The merit-aware approach resulted in modest gains for Hispanic and Native American applicants.

42. *Id.* at 40.

Table 3: Application of the Merit-Aware Approach in Selective University—Diverse Campus[43]

Ethnic Group	Applicant Pool (%)	Percent w/ SAT ≥ 1160 (A)	Percent in Merit Group (B)	Percent in Screened Pool (A+B)
American Indian	0.5	0.1	0.4	0.2
Asian	4.8	7.8	4.5	7.0
Black	5.9	2.0	12.1	4.5
Foreign National	0.2	0.4	0.2	0.3
Hispanic	3.3	2.2	2.7	2.3
Other American	1.8	1.2	2.0	1.4
White	81.9	82.9	77.6	81.5
Not specified	1.6	3.4	0.4	2.7

Table 3 illustrates how a campus can lose diversity ground if it focuses solely on SAT scores. Overall diverse representation decreases by a full percentage point with an SAT cutoff of 1160. Specifically, with respect to African American candidates, an SAT-only approach results in decreasing black representation by two-thirds from the original applicant pool (5.9 percent) to the screened-applicant pool (2 percent). The merit index alone, however, creates a pool with 12.1 percent African American and 22 percent minority representation.[44]

Conclusion

In 1964, President Johnson challenged the nation to see the inherent unfairness in centuries of institutional discrimination and the need for intentional measures to level the playing field, so every American could have unfettered access to educational and economic opportunities. Affirmative action programs established the floor for how the government, businesses, and

43. *Id.* at 41.
44. *Id.*

educational institutions could right past wrongs. But affirmative action was only the floor, and organizations (places of higher education, in this instance) could and can do more. Merit-aware admissions processes like the Achievement Framework promoted by Professor Taylor could have a lasting and profound impact on the ability of law schools to improve diversity. But this alone does not address merit in our admissions process. Visionary legal minds created the LSAT almost 70 years ago in an environment far less diverse and far more discouraging to diversity than where we are today.

It is time for the ABA, law schools, law firms, and corporate legal departments to collaborate on creating an admissions process that, to echo President Johnson, accounts for the challenges people overcome and provides for unfettered access to pursue opportunity in line with their abilities and ambitions. This is a true meritocracy. And it does not end with the law school admissions process but continues with how law firms recruit, evaluate their associates, and make promotion decisions. The final chapter addresses these critical decision points and how tradition, bias, and homophily are albatrosses prevalent in society that also impact diversity and inclusion efforts in law firms.

CHAPTER 6

Hurdles: Tradition, Homophily, and Bias

Hope is not blind optimism. It's not ignoring the enormity of the task ahead or the roadblocks that stand in our path. It's not sitting on the sidelines or shirking from a fight. Hope is that thing inside us that insists, despite all evidence to the contrary, that something better awaits us if we have the courage to reach for it, and work for it, and fight for it.

–President Barack Obama

Tradition and bias. Both hinder law firms' diversity efforts. Law firms stubbornly cling to an antiquated recruiting process, working against their stated goal and best efforts to have more diverse recruiting classes. And, as several examples from a variety of contexts will show later in this chapter, unconscious bias is ubiquitous, so it should come as no surprise that it also impacts whom law firms retain and ultimately elect to their partnerships. Law firms cannot control the consequences of institutionalized inequality resulting in a lingering educational achievement gap that disqualifies many children from ever being viable law school candidates and eventually lawyers. However, firms can control how they pursue underrepresented law students and the opportunities they receive upon entering legal practice. This chapter explores both.

A 20th-Century Recruiting Model in the 21st Century: The First Hurdle

Professor Lauren Rivera's groundbreaking book, *Pedigree: How Elite Students Get Elite Jobs*,[1] argues that how law firms (and other "elite" employers) define and evaluate merit in their hiring practices advantages people from affluent backgrounds, resulting in a class ceiling. According to Rivera, employers evaluate candidates' social networks and intellect on their extracurricular and leisure activities; evaluators receive little guidance on how to systematically judge merit; and the most viable candidates attend schools with preexisting ties to top firms (and, for the most part, applications received at diversity fairs are not taken seriously). Professor Rivera's research examined top-tier law firms, investment banks, and consulting firms, and Professor William Henderson of Indiana University School of Law has focused specifically on the legal profession. Henderson set out to determine if heavy reliance on law school pedigree results in a better candidate pool. His research in the area brought him to this conclusion: nope.

In "Solving the Legal Profession's Diversity Problem,"[2] Professor Henderson analyzes law firms' overreliance on tradition in its recruiting practices. For generations, law firms have preferred students from the most selective law schools because students attending these schools endured a rigorous vetting process—as shown in Chapter 5, elite schools traditionally exclusively admit students with the highest undergraduate grade point averages (UGPAs) and Law School Admissions Test (LSAT) scores—and many of the people making the hiring decisions are alumni of these schools. Law firms' overreliance on recruiting students from elite schools is misguided and hurts their long-stated goal of promoting diversity in the legal profession. Henderson describes lawyers as a "highly filtered" population because to become a practicing attorney one must obtain a four-year degree, score high enough on the LSAT to attend an American Bar Association (ABA)-accredited law school, complete law school, and pass a state bar examination. That means these people are highly motivated and smart. Or, as psychologists would say, lawyers belong to a "range-restricted" population because, compared to the general population, this is a group with high cognitive ability that has endured a rigorous weeding-out process.

---

1. Lauren A. Rivera, Pedigree: How Elite Students Get Elite Jobs (2015).
2. William D. Henderson, *Solving the Legal Profession's Diversity Problem*, PD Q., Feb. 2016, at 23.

Because lawyers choose a profession designed to weed people out, Henderson researched the correlation between undergraduate GPAs, LSAT scores, law school grades, and a person's long-term success as a practicing attorney. Henderson relied on research conducted by Professors Marjorie Shultz and Sheldon Zedeck of the University of California (UC), Berkeley for empirical data.[3]

The Shultz-Zedeck study identified 26 lawyer effectiveness factors as provided by industrial and organizational psychology research on attorneys. The professors created a survey to measure lawyer effectiveness on each of the 26 factors on a scale of 1 to 5 and evaluated more than 1,000 UC Berkeley and UC Hastings law alumni and approximately 200 UC Berkeley law students. Shultz and Zedeck measured the participants' scale ratings against their undergraduate GPAs, LSAT scores, and law school grades.

The results included the following findings:

- For law school graduates, there was a modest, positive correlation between grades and LSAT scores and factors such as analysis and reasoning, researching the law, writing, and problem solving.
- There was a statistically significant negative correlation between first-year grades and LSAT scores, and networking and community service. In the law student sample, there was no positive correlation between undergraduate GPA and any of the 26 effectiveness factors.
- Undergraduate GPA had a negative association with practical judgment, seeing the world through the eyes of others, developing relationships, integrity, and community service.

The Schultz-Zedeck study also assessed various job-relevant indicators of future lawyer success that cannot be captured by relying solely on academic factors. They compared the participants' survey ratings against performance on the Hogan Personality Inventory (HPI), a widely used personality assessment tool that is deemed a better indicator for lawyer effectiveness than other tools. The HPI measures personality traits that include confidence, composure under pressure, initiative, desire for leadership roles, extraversion, tact, self-discipline, creative potential, and achievement orientation. Shultz and Zedeck identified correlations between the HPI and the survey they created that suggest law firms

3. Kristen Holmquist, *The Shultz-Zedeck Research on Law School Admissions*, 63 J. Legal Educ. 565 (2014).

should focus less on school pedigree and more on job-relevant behavior when recruiting candidates. Furthermore, their research did not reveal performance gaps based on race and gender with respect to lawyer effectiveness.

Henderson concludes the following from his research and the Shultz-Zedeck study:

- Lawyers do not need to attend elite law schools to succeed in law firms.
- The correlation between law school grades and future law firm performance has more to do with individual motivation than pedigree.
- More law school graduates have the aptitude to become high-performing partners than most law firm partners think.
- Law firms will see a more diverse and higher-performing candidate pool if they place less emphasis on academic pedigree and more on job-relevant factors.

Homophily and Unconscious Bias: More Hurdles

Let us assume that law firms adopt race- and gender-neutral recruiting strategies; that will not impact how law firms retain and ultimately promote diverse partnership classes. People who stay and succeed in law firms are those who receive career-boosting opportunities. But a certain amount of attrition is built into the law firm business model, and lawyers of color attrite at disproportionately higher rates than everyone else. So how can law firms stem the attrition of people of color? Henderson references a study by professors from Penn State University and Massachusetts Institute of Technology that shows a correlation between associates receiving (and doing well on) high-quality work and achieving long-term success in their firms. This type of work generally comes from influential partners and provides junior lawyers with additional exposure to these partners and reputation-building opportunities.[4]

Henderson's research on diversity and the work-assignment process does not reveal systemic gender or racial bias. However, he does acknowledge that associates and partners may naturally gravitate toward people like themselves, which disadvantages women and minority associates because there are so few

4. Henderson, *supra* note 2, at 30.

women and minority partners positioned to dole out career-advancing opportunities. Social psychologists refer to the concept of people gravitating toward people similar to themselves as "homophily." Moreover, research published in *Perspectives on Psychological Science* states in-group favoritism is a bigger motivator than overt hostility toward the out-group, resulting in in-group preferential treatment benefiting majority groups and working to the disadvantage of minority groups. Unfortunately, homophily has far-reaching consequences, as illustrated by the disparate examples that follow.[5]

Pedestrians and Drivers

In *Racial Bias in Driver Yielding Behavior at Crosswalks*, Tara Goddard and Kimberly Barsamian Kahn of Portland State University and Arlie Adkins of the University of Arizona set out to determine why it is more likely for black and Hispanic male pedestrians to suffer a fatal injury than their white counterparts.[6] According to the Centers for Disease Control and Prevention, the pedestrian fatality rates for black and Hispanic men were twice the rate of white men from 2000 to 2010.[7] The researchers concluded that drivers' racial attitudes and biases influence their interactions with pedestrians.

Pedestrian treatment depends largely on who the pedestrian is. Research in this area reveals that pedestrians' visible characteristics influence how drivers treat them. For example, drivers are more willing to yield for visibly disabled pedestrians (e.g., people with canes or in wheelchairs). A study of Israeli drivers revealed a preference for drivers to yield to pedestrians perceived to be in their own age group. Socioeconomic status also influences driving behavior because drivers of luxury cars were least likely to yield to pedestrians. The conclusion drawn from these results: yielding behavior is a courtesy or privilege granted by drivers and not something dictated by traffic laws adhered to by drivers.[8]

5. Evan P. Apfelbaum et al., *Rethinking the Baseline in Diversity Research: Should We Be Explaining the Effects of Homogeneity?*, 9 Persp. on Psychol. Sci. 235–44 (2014).

6. Tara Goddard et al., National Institute for Transportation and Communities, Racial Bias in Driver Yielding Behavior at Crosswalks (2014), https://pdxscholar.library.pdx.edu/cgi/viewcontent.cgi?referer=https://www.bing.com/&httpsredir=1&article=1009&context=psy_fac.

7. *Id.* at 3.

8. *Id.* at 4.

To determine if bias resulted in disproportionately higher fatality rates for black and Hispanic pedestrians, Portland State University researchers created a controlled field experiment to observe the interaction between pedestrians and drivers of different races at a marked crosswalk. They based their analysis on three factors: (1) whether the first approaching car stopped for the pedestrian (a trained member of the research team); (2) the number of cars that passed before the pedestrian could cross; and (3) how long the pedestrian waited before crossing.

The pedestrians were three white and three black research team members in their 20s who were about the same height and weight and wore identical outfits. The researchers conducted trials over five days in the fall of 2013 under clear weather conditions during off-peak traffic hours at an unsignalized midblock crosswalk in downtown Portland, Oregon, near Portland State University with frequent driver-pedestrian encounters. The black and white pedestrians alternated turns crossing the street and timed their arrival at the crosswalk to coincide with the first set of cars passing a marked spot approximately 300 feet from the crosswalk, after being stopped at a traffic light. Pedestrians signaled their intention to cross by stepping toward the curb, positioning their bodies toward oncoming traffic, making eye contact whenever possible, and staying on the curb until the driver yielded. Researchers timed each trial beginning when the driver passed the designated mark and ending when the pedestrian reached the other side of the street after walking a normal pace.

The study concluded that drivers were less likely to stop for black pedestrians than for white pedestrians and that black pedestrians waited significantly longer to cross the street safely. When viewed from the perspective of black pedestrians, it is not a stretch to assume that longer wait times and the inability to cross the street may be perceived as the driver behaving in an aggressive or discourteous manner resulting in discomfort and inconvenience for black pedestrians. The cumulative effect of these experiences, according to the researchers, could result in minorities attempting to cross in unsafe conditions, hence the disproportionately higher fatality rate for black and Hispanic pedestrians.

The National Basketball Association

In 2007, the National Bureau of Economic Research published an article entitled "Racial Discrimination among NBA Referees," studying the impact of race-based implicit bias on how referees officiate National Basketball Association (NBA) games.[9] The NBA provided the ideal situation to analyze taste-based discrimination because referees make split-second decisions in high-pressure forums, NBA officials (according to former NBA Commissioner David Stern) are among the most scrutinized employees in the world due to constant monitoring and regular performance feedback, referees and players are engaged in repeated interactions throughout the course of 48-minute games, and the NBA arbitrarily assigns officiating crews for each basketball game. Researchers sought to determine the impact of these factors on the number of fouls called against black versus white players.

The study included several notable findings. First, there was systemic evidence of own-race bias where players earned approximately 4 percent fewer fouls or scored 2.5 more points when they are the positive recipients of own-race bias; second, refereeing bias can impact the outcome of games based on the racial composition of officiating crew; and third, own-race bias is prevalent across all referees, with black officials having a greater propensity to call more fouls on white players, and white officials having a greater propensity to call more fouls on black players.

In 2014, the Brookings Institute released a report examining the impact of implicit bias in officiating NBA games.[10] The report agreed with the 2007 findings of race-based bias among NBA officials, but found that seven years later the bias disappeared in the wake of the negative media coverage surrounding the report. The Brookings Institute researches examined several potential explanations for this outcome and concluded that the most likely explanation was that referees changed their behavior after becoming aware of their biases.

Financial Markets

Researchers sought to determine the impact of in-group bias on financial markets. Professors from the University of Miami, University of Mannheim, and

9. Joseph Price & Justin Wolfers, National Bureau of Economic Research, Working Paper No. 13206, Racial Discrimination among NBA Referees (2007), http://www.nber.org/papers/w13206.pdf.

10. Devin G. Pope et al., Brookings Institution, Awareness Reduces Racial Bias (2014), https://www.brookings.edu/wp-content/uploads/2016/06/awareness_reduces_racial_bias_wolfers.pdf.

University of Michigan concluded that in-group bias does exist and that the economic consequences from it could be considerable.[11] Their study explored the impact of in-group bias on the forecasts of sell-side equity analysts with respect to quarterly earnings of publicly traded companies and those companies' actual announcement returns. The study examined if male analysts had systemically lower earnings estimates for women-led firms; if domestic analysts underestimated earnings for firms led by foreign chief executive officers (CEOs); and if political affiliation also resulted in in-group bias. The study concluded that analysts have a more favorable opinion of CEOs who are like themselves—overwhelmingly Republican American white men.

Their results found that firms led by women CEOs received systemically lower earnings forecasts than firms headed by men. Consequently, women-led firms had more positive and less negative earnings surprises than firms led by men. The researchers refined the analysis to focus exclusively on male analysts and revealed that male consensus forecasts for women-led firms were lower than their consensus forecasts for firms led by men. The gender-related in-group bias remained even after the researchers used different firm-specific control variables to examine the forecast bias. They also found that women analysts relative to men analysts generally had less disagreement about earnings of firms headed by women CEOs. Because 80 percent of analysts are men, the market responds more favorably to women-led firms because most of their earnings forecasts are lower than their actual earnings announcements.

Researchers attributed this to how in-group bias inhibited the ability of analysts who are disproportionately domestic and Republican to objectively evaluate firms led by foreign and Democratic CEOs—people not representing the analysts' in-group. Consequently, firms headed by foreign and Democratic CEOs experience systematically upward-biased earnings surprises. "These results are also reflected in analysts' buy and sell recommendations, with systematically more buy and sell recommendations for stocks of firms headed by CEOs belonging to their in-group."[12]

The research was based on literature addressing the economics of discrimination, which explores alternative explanations for majority-minority

11. Sima Jannati et al., In-Group Bias in Financial Markets (2018), https://papers.ssrn.com/sol3/papers.cfm?abstract_id=2884218.

12. *Id.* at 2.

disparities. For example, demographic characteristics such as gender, ethnicity, or political orientation become markers for other unobservable characteristics such as competence or expertise. Economists describe this form of decision making as "statistical discrimination" leading to systematically different treatment of people with otherwise similar observable characteristics. Further study in this area by labor economists suggests that decision makers will find ways to distinguish people if there are no observable differences, resulting in an illogical link between observable or known characteristics (e.g., race, gender, national origin, or political affiliation) and expectations surrounding a person's abilities.

As we have seen earlier, in-group favoritism affects how much courtesy drivers show to pedestrians, how many fouls referees call on NBA players, and how much profit analysts predict for firms. In-group favoritism is ubiquitous and also impacts law firms.

The Legal Profession

Dr. Arin Reeves's *Written in Black and White: Exploring Confirmation Bias in Racialized Perceptions of Writing Skills*[13] explores how bias influences the way law firm partners evaluate the written work product of junior lawyers. Dr. Reeves conducted a study where she asked lawyers from various law firms to review a memorandum drafted by two fictional male third-year associates named Thomas Meyer. Both graduated from New York University Law School with credentials strong enough to earn employment in a major law firm. The only difference between the associates was their race—one was black and the other was white. The memo included a combination of 22 errors of fact, grammar, and analysis. Reeves and her team asked 60 partners to edit the memo as part of a study on "writing competencies for young lawyers." The partners were asked to rate the overall quality of the memo on a 1 (extremely poor) to 5 (extremely well written) scale. Fifty-three partners participated in the study, with 29 evaluating white Thomas Meyer's memo and 24 evaluating black Thomas Meyer's memo.

13. Arin N. Reeves, Nextions, Written in Black and White: Exploring Confirmation Bias in Racialized Perceptions of Writing Skills (2014).

The following are the quantitative findings of the same memo drafted by a fictional black and a fictional white associate evaluated by 53 law firm partners:[14]

- Overall ratings
  - 4.1/5.0 for "Caucasian" Thomas
  - 3.2/5.0 for "African American" Thomas
- Grammatical errors found
  - An average of 2.9/7.0 for "Caucasian" Thomas
  - An average of 5.8/7.0 for "African American" Thomas
- Technical writing errors found
  - An average of 4.1/6.0 for "Caucasian" Thomas
  - An average of 4.9/6.0 for "African American" Thomas
- Errors in fact found
  - An average of 3.2/5.0 for "Caucasian" Thomas
  - An average of 3.9/5.0 for "African American" Thomas

The following are the qualitative findings:

- White Thomas Meyer
  - "Generally a good writer but needs to work on . . ."
  - "Has potential"
  - "Good analytical skills"
- Black Thomas Meyer
  - "Needs a lot of work"
  - "Can't believe he went to NYU"
  - "Average at best"[15]

This study is significant for several reasons, specifically because possessing effective written and oral communication skills is among the core competencies by which lawyers are judged. Therefore, we cannot underestimate how even the perception of being deficient in these skills can significantly impact the careers of young lawyers where their performance is scrutinized by the partners they work for and the clients they serve. We must not, however, interpret Dr. Reeves's study to reflect the experiences of all African American

14. *Id.* at 4–5.
15. *Id.*

associates and the sentiments of all partners reviewing their written work product. Some associates of color are succeeding and staying at law firms long enough to be considered for partnership, but they must still contend with the consequences of bias as they attempt to build their practices.

In "Which Path to Power? Workplace Networks and the Relative Effectiveness of Inheritance and Rainmaking Strategies for Professional Partners," Professors Forrest Briscoe and Andrew von Nordenflycht sought to determine how inheriting someone's practice or building your own (rainmaking) impacted partners' careers in professional services firms.[16] Both strategies rely on a partner's ability to establish meaningful internal and external relationships that position him or her for long-term success to eventually generate client revenue. Because professional services require the application of customized knowledge to client problems, it is difficult for clients to assess the quality of the service either before or after it has been performed. As a result, according to Briscoe and von Nordenflycht, clients base the decision to retain a lawyer on at least two factors: their ability to trust the attorney based on that person's reputation for providing quality work and social relationships that have developed over time between senior client executives and individual partners in the firm.

The inability to assess work quality effectively means that clients will continue working almost exclusively with the lawyer with whom they have always worked. This dynamic makes the rainmaking strategy incredibly difficult, but not impossible, and the inheritance strategy depends entirely on the senior partner's desire to pass off his (because they are mostly men) practice to a highly regarded protégé. Based on homophily, that is likely to be someone from a background similar to that of the senior partner—which typically excludes people of color, women, and people who are openly gay.

The obvious question: how do we combat implicit bias and its consequences? As we saw with the NBA referees, raising awareness of the issue can change behavior and many organizations have introduced programs that address bias and its impact on their systems. But raising awareness is not

16. Forrest Briscoe & Andrew von Nordenflycht, *Which Path to Power? Workplace Networks and the Relative Effectiveness of Inheritance and Rainmaking Strategies for Professional Partners*, 1 J. Profs. & Org. 33 (2014), *available at* http://www.personal.psu.edu/fsb10/papers/Briscoe_von_Nordenflycht_2014_JPO_Which_Path_to_Power.pdf.

enough; intentional measures must be taken to root it out. The NeuroLeadership Institute (NLI) uses neuroscience research that explores these issues and develops solutions to help organizations to better understand and to ultimately eliminate the harmful effects of bias—"cognitive quirks" influencing our world view and decision making. In "Beyond Bias: Neuroscience Research Shows How New Organizational Practices Can Shift Ingrained Thinking,"[17] authors Heidi Grant Halvorson and David Rock of the NLI determined there are approximately 150 known biases that can be broken down into five categories: similarity, expedience, experience, distance, and safety (NLI refers to these as SEEDS).

The preceding examples regarding driver-pedestrian interactions, NBA referees, financial analysts, and the partner review of the same legal memo drafted by a black and a white associate reveal similarity bias—the belief that something must be right because it feels right. Similarity bias is the brain's way of promoting and/or protecting people similar to themselves and manifests in two ways: in-group bias and out-group bias. In-group bias occurs when people automatically have a more favorable opinion of people of, for example, the same race, ethnicity, religion, socioeconomic status, or profession. Out-group bias is just the opposite—having a less favorable opinion of people different from themselves. Similarity bias relates directly to drivers being more courteous to pedestrians similar to themselves, referees calling more fouls on players of an opposite race, financial analysts undervaluing the performances of companies led by people different from themselves, senior lawyers evaluating associates in a certain way, and clients hiring particular lawyers to represent them.

Leaders See Hurdles and Remove Them

In *Breaking Through: The Making of Minority Executives in Corporate America*, Professor David Thomas of Harvard Business School states minorities in corporate settings are often overlooked for promotions because people tend to view members of their own racial groups as more promotable, and often give them higher performance ratings. Consequently, high-performing

17. Heidi Grant Halvorson & David Rock, *Beyond Bias: Neuroscience Research Shows How New Organizational Practices Can Shift Ingrained Thinking*, Strategy & Bus., Autumn 2015.

minorities "remain comparatively invisible in the selection process."[18] Organizations wanting to improve diversity in their senior ranks recognize this glass ceiling as a problem, and take proactive steps to ensure a level playing field by having influential senior executives (usually a white man) sponsor promising underrepresented minorities. Thomas's research found that intentional measures to involve senior executives in boosting the careers of promising minorities demonstrates leadership's personal investment in promoting diversity to the entire organization, and helped convince minorities they had a real opportunity at attaining senior executive status because leaders took deliberate steps. The lack of visible diversity also impacts perceptions of how far people think they can excel in an organization.

Statistics reveal a general lack of diversity in the legal profession and invisibility of lawyers of color in the promotion process. According to the ABA, the legal profession is 88 percent white, and people of color represent 10 percent of all partners in the largest law firms. A Microsoft Corporation report contrasted the representation of black lawyers against other professions. For example, African Americans represent 4.2 percent of the legal profession and constitute 9.8 percent of accountants/auditors, 8.5 percent of financial managers, and 7.1 percent of physicians/surgeons.[19] The June 2014 edition of the *American Lawyer* painted an even bleaker picture for law firms in "The Diversity Crisis: Big Firms' Continuing Failure." In 2013, one in 54 partners (1.9 percent) were African American and 0.5 percent (one in 170) were black women.[20]

Many law firms work tirelessly to support and improve the diverse representation of lawyers, but most of their efforts focus on recruiting—which has its challenges as mentioned earlier in this chapter—but equal if not more attention should address its most difficult area: retaining and promoting people of color. In this respect, law firms can learn from the U.S. military and the National Football League—two very disparate employers that have been

18. David A. Thomas & John J. Gabarro, Breaking Through: The Making of Minority Executives in Corporate America 28 (1999).

19. Jeffrey Meisner, *Raising the Bar: Exploring the Diversity Gap within the Legal Profession*, Microsoft, Dec. 10, 2013, https://blogs.technet.microsoft.com/microsoft_on_the_issues/2013/12/10/raising-the-bar-exploring-the-diversity-gap-within-the-legal-profession/.

20. Julie Triedman, *The Diversity Crisis: Big Firms' Continuing Failure*, Am. Law., May 29, 2014, https://www.law.com/americanlawyer/almID/1202656372552/The-Diversity-Crisis-Big-Firms-Continuing-Failure/.

intentional in cultivating a robust talent pool to ensure they keep and promote the very best people. What these employers have in common is that their leaders played and continue to play a direct role in tackling the most challenging aspects of their respective diversity efforts. While none of these leaders specifically identified unconscious bias or homophily impediments, they knew *something* was not right.

The U.S. military recognized that minority officers were not afforded the same opportunities for career advancement as white officers, and addressed this by taking deliberate and targeted measures. General Eric Shinseki, former chief of staff of the Army, ordered the service to conduct a study identifying the root cause of the lack of minority general officers. In 2006, the Joint Center for Political and Economic Studies published a report that found, in part, that minorities were significantly underrepresented in combat arms branches—the largest pipeline for promotion to general officer ranks.[21] The Army then took steps to ensure that minority officers were at least being considered for this branch, and began to aggressively recruit them for combat arms positions.

The American Forces Press Service reported that Admiral Mike Mullen, former chairman of the Joint Chiefs of Staff, took similar steps to ensure that minorities had the opportunity to compete for admiral, the Navy's highest officer rank. Admiral Mullen once said: "We know how to make [general officers] . . . we've been doing it a long time . . . You put [people] in the right jobs, and if they do well they get promoted."[22] So, in 2005, when he became chief of naval operations, Admiral Mullen made increasing diversity a top priority and changed the assignment process to ensure that more minorities were being considered for positions that put them on the senior leadership track. Admiral Mullen created accountability by requiring his direct reports (other senior officers) to update him regularly on their progress.

Over the past decade, the National Football League (NFL) also took deliberate steps to promote diversity that resulted in eight of the league's 32 teams being led by men of color at the beginning of the 2017 season. This is

21. Anthony D. Reyes, Joint Center for Political and Economic Studies, Strategic Options for Managing Diversity in the U.S. Army (2006), http://www.dtic.mil/dtic/tr/fulltext/u2/a493839.pdf.

22. Karen Parrish, *Mullen: U.S. Military Needs More Diversity*, U.S. Dep't Def., Oct. 18, 2010, http://archive.defense.gov/news/newsarticle.aspx?id=61315.

significant: by contrast, between 1920 and 2000, only six of 400 NFL head coaching positions were held by African Americans.[23] In *Advancing the Ball: Race, Reformation, and the Quest for Equal Coaching Opportunity in the NFL*, Professor N. Jeremi Duru of American University Washington College of Law chronicles the path the NFL took to increased diversity. In 2003, the NFL received significant criticism for its hiring practices when only two teams were led by black coaches. The late Johnnie Cochran threatened a race discrimination lawsuit against the league, resulting in the creation of a diversity committee led by the Pittsburgh Steelers owner, the late Dan Rooney, to examine the league's hiring practices and to make recommendations.

Rooney's diversity committee concluded the NFL was the consummate good old boys' club, and owners and other top-level executives based hiring decisions partly on relationships. African Americans seeking head coaching positions did not have access to or relationships with people making the hiring decisions and, as a result, were not viable candidates for getting the job. The NFL had to make these invisible candidates visible, so Rooney's group found a way for owners to gain exposure to untapped coaching talent. They recommended that each team consider at least one candidate of color for every head coaching vacancy and suggested that the league impose a fine on teams that did not comply. The NFL adopted this proposal, which later became known as the Rooney Rule. The Rooney Rule represents progress, but full equality has not been reached. In an October 2017 Bloomberg article, Ira Boudway stated that African American player representation hovers around 70 percent for the past two decades but representation of coaches of color has never surpassed 25 percent in the league's history.[24] These statistics should not discourage us but should serve as a reminder that this work requires persistence, creativity, and honesty about bias as an impediment to change.

While the military and NFL are quite different from the legal profession, there are transferrable lessons to be learned. First, the military acknowledged certain jobs better position people for promotion than others; the same holds true for law firms. Viable partnership candidates receive and excel at

23. N. Jeremi Duru, Advancing the Ball: Race, Reformation, and the Quest for Equal Coaching Opportunity in the NFL (2011).

24. Ira Boudway, *NFL Diversity Report Shows Small Gains for Black Coaches, GMs*, Bloomberg, Oct. 18, 2017, https://www.bloomberg.com/news/articles/2017-10-18/nfl-diversity-report-shows-small-gains-for-black-coaches-gms.

career-boosting opportunities (e.g., work for an institutional client generating a lot of revenue). And second, the NFL's Rooney Rule drives home the importance of exposure and visibility to influential decision makers. Just like all work is not created equally, law firm partners are not either. Serious partner prospects either work for a powerful partner or at a minimum have established a reputation as a lieutenant for a powerful partner who can make them a partner. Similar to the military and the NFL, intentional measures are necessary for law firms to make progress at retaining and promoting the very best lawyers.

The first step is to acknowledge that something in the current process is not working. As mentioned previously, bias influences how lawyers evaluate the work product of black and white associates and whom clients hire to work on their matters, both of which influence a lawyer's business case for partnership consideration. The business case is also determined by lawyers' relationships with clients and senior lawyers' willingness to give them work. Professor David Wilkins of Harvard Law School and G. Mitu Gulati of Duke University found that this system disadvantages minorities for two reasons: (1) they are less likely than whites to have relationships with in-house counsel who can give them business; and (2) the internal market is built on reciprocity, so other lawyers may be less inclined to give work to minorities who typically have less access to well-paying clients.[25] Law firms and their clients can fix this problem.

First, law firms committed to advancing diversity and inclusion can use this as an opportunity to improve how they identify and cultivate talent. The law firm business model is built on attrition and many junior lawyers entering firms do not want to become partners. Absent deliberate measures to identify and develop talent, law firms will lose people they want to keep—and that goes for every demographic group. But the lack of critical mass of lawyers of color makes this a real challenge for improving diversity in the partnership ranks. Firms should approach career development issues with a diversity lens. Like the military, law firms have been promoting partners since their inception, so they know what it takes to promote people—pair promising associates with

25. David B. Wilkins & G. Mitu Gulati, *Why Are There So Few Black Lawyers in Corporate Law Firms? An Institutional Analysis*, 84 Cal. L. Rev. 493 (1996).

influential partners who can dole out career-boosting work, facilitate connections to other influential partners and institutional clients, and, when the time comes, advocate for the associates' election to the partnership. Annual performance reviews could be used to identify junior lawyers demonstrating potential for long-term success and senior partners who play the sponsorship role described earlier.

Sponsorship is not a novel concept; it has existed informally in law firms since the beginning of the legal profession. For generations, junior lawyers learned the practice of law from senior attorneys who, over time, gave them more responsibility and eventually direct access and exposure to clients. These senior lawyers also sponsored their protégés during the partnership election process. The apprentice model present in the early days of the legal profession may not be feasible in today's large law firm with hundreds if not thousands of lawyers, so many firms have formal training and mentoring programs to fill the void. While these programs may be effective, there is no substitute for learning at the side of an experienced lawyer with the influence to position a lawyer for long-term success. This was true during the apprenticeship days of the profession and remains so today because associates who become partners have sponsors. Every sponsor can be a mentor, but not every mentor has the gravitas to be a sponsor.

Serious conversations about the business case for promotion occur when associates are within a year or two of partnership consideration. As a result, sponsorship relationships must develop much earlier. Because the lawyer evaluation process is frequently a ranking system, an early misstep can eliminate a junior lawyer from ever gaining an advocate to help his or her career advance within the firm. As Dr. Reeves's writing study reveals, unconscious bias irrationally and negatively influences how people evaluate the abilities of African American associates, so it may be harder for these lawyers to recover from a mistake because it may subconsciously confirm for some that black associates are not as capable as whites. The converse of this "one-mistake rule" is the halo effect: a junior lawyer impresses a partner by providing outstanding work in early assignments; the partner tells his or her colleagues, and the junior lawyer becomes known as a superstar. Associates with the halo are not subject to the one-mistake rule because their missteps are considered anomalies. They also have enough supporters in their corner to help them overcome any potential obstacles that may arise from their mistake (obviously depending on the magnitude). Bias also affects who receives the halo, since cognitive associations reinforce preconceived beliefs (i.e., with all things being equal, the partner evaluating two associates may be more inclined to see superstar potential in the associate of his same race). This is not to suggest that the halo is not deserved or earned, but just that unconscious bias may eliminate certain lawyers from being deemed worthy of a halo, which reduces their chances of receiving sponsors organically.

Second, clients can use their influence to help law firms improve diversity. In 2016, Microsoft and other legal departments endorsed the passage of ABA Resolution 113, which created the ABA Model Diversity Survey. The ABA created the survey to help legal departments hold law firms accountable by requesting diversity statistics regarding recruitment, attrition, promotion, leadership composition, compensation data, and a breakdown of fees billed to the client along identity groups. The survey provides clients a standardized format to annually track law firm diversity progress on key metrics.

The significance of the ABA Model Diversity Survey cannot be understated: it combines the influence, reach, and credibility of the ABA and the power of paying clients to affect law firm behavior in promoting diversity and inclusion. Furthermore, it opens the door for legal departments to proactively address how bias may impact their approach to hiring outside counsel by creating an additional layer of accountability. As the study by Professors Briscoe and von Nordenflycht reveals, clients base hiring decisions on at least two factors: a lawyer's reputation for good work and social relationships that develop over time. Homophily and unconscious bias can disadvantage underrepresented lawyers on both fronts and there is nothing a survey can do to fix this. However, to boost the careers of promising underrepresented lawyers working on their matters, clients could intentionally give challenging work directly to them and sing their lawyer's praises to the relationship partner. These two simple steps could go a long way in elevating the prospects of these lawyers, while demonstrating the client's commitment to diversity and simultaneously partnering with law firms to create a more diverse partnership. This approach strengthens the firm's relationship with the client, positions people often overlooked in the partnership process for long-term success, and makes the promotion of diversity and inclusion a shared responsibility of clients and law firms.

Conclusion

An often-stated law firm goal is to reflect the diversity of the nation. This is laudatory, but it is merely aspirational and unachievable if we fail to reckon with and attempt to correct what holds us back. There is power in the amalgamation of races and ethnicities that make up our nation, but the inability to talk honestly about the role race and racism have played and currently play in society is a weakness. As referenced in Chapters 3 and 4, the founders of public education intentionally built the system on inequality and *Plessy v. Ferguson,*[26] and other laws grounded in racism exacerbated the situation. Educational inequity was institutionalized, and lawyers fought gallantly to end it. This fight, however, could not wipe away the damage from unequal access to opportunity that created a legacy that persists today.

In our nation's almost 250 years of existence, laws promoting fairness in the pursuit of opportunity are less than 60 years old. Most Baby Boomers and all of their parents lived through segregation and institutionalized educational inequality. The divergent experiences of Americans based on race resulted in lasting economic and educational ramifications. As noted in Chapter 3, stark differences exist in wealth accumulation between black and white families based on the educational achievement of the preceding generation of their parents. These differences impact where people live, the schools their children attend, and the quality of the education children receive based on the resources available to them. A consequence is that some children get a head start in the contest for entry into the legal profession because they have been training for it their entire educational careers, while others are unwittingly playing a game of catch-up. This results in a thin, leaky diversity pipeline for the legal profession beginning with early education. This is compounded by law schools' overreliance on an entrance exam that inhibits diversity, the law firms' stubborn devotion to a 20th-century recruiting process that has not stood up to scrutiny for providing an accurate measure of the likelihood of candidate success, and the pervasiveness of bias influencing how law firms assess ability and worthiness for partnership consideration. Progress will occur when decision makers acknowledge the existence and damaging consequences of these issues and look for 21st-century solutions to adequately address them.

26. Plessy v. Ferguson, 163 U.S. 537 (1896).

As we have seen in this chapter and previous chapters, change happens when visionary leaders and average people set out to make a difference. Branch Rickey was astute enough to recognize his power to change the status quo, but also humble enough to know he did not fully grasp all the issues. He chose to become a student of race and race relations to be effective in pursuing integration. There were a lot of great black baseball players but few Branch Rickeys—leaders willing to acknowledge the inherent unfairness and missed business opportunities in discriminating against African American athletes. Major League Baseball adhered to a tradition of racial discrimination that directly impacted the business. Rickey bucked tradition when he signed Jackie Robinson and other teams eventually followed in his footsteps

Harriet Tubman embodies the power of diversity and inclusion: an intelligent, courageous, diminutive, formerly enslaved black woman who led men during the Civil War. If I asked you to close your eyes and visualize a leader, someone resembling Harriet Tubman probably would not come to mind. This is implicit bias. It limits our ability to see potential in others because we may not associate them with being an Army general, an NFL head coach, or a law firm partner. And homophily perpetuates this cycle because it confines the dissemination of career-boosting opportunities to people of similar backgrounds. Fortunately, research in social psychology provides tools to identify bias and to root it out. But this is not enough. A law firm wanting to create a true meritocracy must account for the toll bias takes on its ability to retain and promote a diverse group of lawyers. Absent this reckoning and deliberate measures to ensure equity in assessing work performance and substantive access and exposure to influential partners and clients, law firms will continue to restrict the talent pool of future law firm partners. We know what impedes progress and have the tools to address it. We just need the courage to fix it.

Closing Remarks

Dear Reader:

If you read the entire book to get to this point, thank you. If you skipped ahead to get here, I appreciate that too. Either way, something compelled you to read beyond the cover! I did not write to tell you how to do diversity and inclusion (D&I). I wrote this book to explore how we have grappled with these issues throughout our nation's history, but conversations about making progress in this area are often divorced from historical context.

The legal profession should reflect the nation because the creation, interpretation, and execution of the law should include diverse viewpoints. In this sense, D&I is of the utmost importance for a profession that has produced central figures in our country's ongoing pursuit of fairness, justice, and equity. As I mentioned in the Prologue and as you now know from reading this book, I don't have all the answers. These issues are difficult, so I will leave you with a few points to consider as you embark on how to make the change you want to see.

First Determine Why D&I Is Important to You and Your Organization

The answer to this question is the foundation for your entire D&I program. I have heard many people simply say "it's the right thing to do." That's true, but that is not enough. Union officers enlisted Harriet Tubman in the South Carolina campaign because her involvement was critical to their mission. A diminutive, formerly enslaved African American woman did not fit the mold of the typical American war hero of the 1800s. But she possessed skills and knowledge the Union Army needed to create and execute a successful operation. Army generals gave Tubman the opportunity to contribute to the Civil War in a way that benefited her and the nation. Are there people in your organization getting overlooked because they have traits dissimilar to current and previous leaders? If so, what can you do to unveil these contributors? D&I is about spreading opportunity in ways that benefit individuals and entire organizations.

Corporate reputation and brand are other issues to consider when determining the importance of this issue to you. Recent events demonstrate the strengthening connection between an institution's D&I commitment and its reputation. President Trump's business council dissolved in part because its chief executive officer members could not take the risk of having their personal and their businesses' reputations associated with the president's inability to unequivocally condemn the actions of white supremacists in Charlottesville, Virginia. Further making this point is the ouster of University of Missouri officials following their inability to fully appreciate the importance of taking swift action to address the hostile environment created by racial insensitivity on campus. Fear of bad press should not motivate your D&I commitment, but you could seek inspiration in making sure you reap all the benefits from having a robust D&I program grounded in your institution's values and business strategy.

Empathic Leaders Modeling Humility, Authenticity, Curiosity, and Courage Can Make a Difference

Jackie Robinson excelled in Major League Baseball because he was great. However, the irrationality of racism could have relegated him to a historical footnote—similar to many talented African American baseball players who preceded him. The prevailing sentiment of the day was that blacks had no place in baseball, and bucking this notion took courage; but courage alone is not enough. You must also have a clear understanding of what you want to solve and the impediments to success. Branch Rickey, a courageous leader, understood both as he embarked on his mission to integrate the nation's pastime.

As I mentioned in Chapter 2, Rickey vowed to combat racism after witnessing the only African American player on his college team sobbing and trying to rub off his black skin after being humiliated multiple times because of his race. This experience gave Rickey empathy and sparked in him an early curiosity regarding the injustices of racism. When Rickey set out on his experiment he recognized that he did not have all the answers, so he became a student of race and racism. He also believed that failure was not an option and he felt obligated to position Robinson for success, because he knew Robinson would not be judged fairly. The stakes for pursuing D&I today are not as high as what Rickey faced, but he exemplifies steps leaders can take when they want to make meaningful, sustainable change. Rickey's story also models President Abraham Lincoln's quote that gets to the heart of courageous leadership: "One is a majority if he is right."

The Legacy of Institutional Racism Casts a Long Shadow

Education is often considered the gateway to better socioeconomic outcomes for people and their families. But the founders of public education did not create it with egalitarianism in mind, and for generations lawyers abetted the creation, passage, and execution of laws that intentionally kept large numbers of Americans undereducated. This is relevant today because the opportunity gaps that exist now are in part due to actions taken decades before, as outlined below.

- In 1776, 13 colonies declared their independence from Great Britain to eventually become the United States of America.
- In 1787, delegates from the southern and northern states determined enslaved African Americans counted as three-fifths of a white American to determine congressional representation and taxes.
- In 1863, the Emancipation Proclamation, an executive order issued by President Lincoln, freed enslaved African Americans in southern states.
- In 1865, the Civil War ended, resulting in the official demise of slavery and the beginnings of trying to piece together a better union for everyone.
- In 1896, the U.S. Supreme Court ruled "separate but equal" constitutional in *Plessy v. Ferguson*,[1] resulting in a racial hierarchy with African Americans occupying the bottom rung.
- In 1954, the Supreme Court ruled "separate but equal" unconstitutional in *Brown v. Board of Education*.[2]

1. Plessy v. Ferguson, 163 U.S. 537 (1896).
2. Brown v. Bd. of Educ., 347 U.S. 483 (1954).

- In 1964, the Civil Rights Act of 1964 made illegal racial segregation and discrimination in workplaces, schools, and public facilities.[3]
- In 1965, President Lyndon B. Johnson signed Executive Order No. 11,246 requiring government contractors take "affirmative action" in hiring minority employees.[4]
- In 1969, President Richard Nixon initiated the "Philadelphia Order" to end the open hostility of craft unions and the construction industry of allowing African Americans "into their closed circle."[5]
- In 1978, in *Regents of the University of California v. Bakke*,[6] the Supreme Court limited the scope of affirmative action policies and ruled unconstitutional the use of "inflexible quotas" in a case involving school admissions practices.[7]

From 1978 until now, affirmative action programs have been under assault despite their original intent to create a fairer society by remedying the consequences of centuries of race-based laws that intentionally limited opportunity. In the *Bakke* dissent, Justice Thurgood Marshall said:

> It must be remembered that, during most of the past 200 years, the Constitution as interpreted by this Court did not prohibit the most ingenious and pervasive forms of discrimination against the Negro. Now, when the state acts to remedy the effects of the legacy of discrimination, I cannot believe that this same Constitution stands as a barrier.[8]

In 2015, the *New Yorker* published an article[9] that captures the current Supreme Court's divergent views on how best to address the legacy of institutional racism. In the 2007 case *Parents Involved in Community Schools v.*

---

3. Laws, *Civil Rights Act of 1964 Explained*, https://civil.laws.com/civil-rights-act-of-1964 (last visited July 15, 2018).

4. Borgna Brunner & Beth Rowen, *Timeline of Affirmative Action Milestones*, Infoplease, https://www.infoplease.com/spot/timeline-affirmative-action-milestones.

5. *Id.*

6. Regents of the Univ. of Cal. v. Bakke, 438 U.S. 265 (1978).

7. Brunner & Rowen, *supra* note 4.

8. Lincoln Caplan, *Thurgood Marshall and the Need for Affirmative Action*, The New Yorker, Dec. 9, 2015, https://www.newyorker.com/news/news-desk/thurgood-marshall-and-the-need-for-affirmative-action.

9. *Id.*

Seattle School District No. 1, Chief Justice Roberts said, "The way to stop discrimination on the basis of race is to stop discriminating on the basis of race."[10] In 2014, Justice Sonia Sotomayor took a different approach when in *Schuette v. Coalition to Defend Affirmative Action, Integration and Immigration Rights, and Fight for Equality by Any Means Necessary* she declared: "The way to stop discrimination on the basis of race is to speak openly and candidly on the subject of race, and to apply the Constitution with eyes wide open to the unfortunate effects of centuries of discrimination."[11]

Chief Justice Roberts's and Justice Sotomayor's divergent positions on how to remedy the legacy of institutional racism cannot be understated. Their views represent those of many Americans. A March 2018 study for the Equality of Opportunity Project provides definitive information on the long-term consequences of racism.[12] This comprehensive study tracked 20 million Americans born between 1978 and 1983 through census and tax records to determine their outcomes as adults. The research compared black and white children raised in similar circumstances and concluded that a black boy raised in a wealthy family is more likely to become poor as an adult than a white boy raised in a wealthy family.[13] The researches made apples-to-apples comparisons and controlled for education levels of the children and their parents and found that black boys have lower outcomes than white boys in 99 percent of the country.

Their research suggests that the most effective way to reduce the black-white gap is to create policies that improve environments within schools and neighborhoods. Targeted mentoring programs accounting for racial inequity, greater social interactions between racial groups, and reduced racial bias may assist in closing the gap.[14] But we must first acknowledge the stubborn persistence and harmful effects of structural institutional racism as a barrier to progress and identify how it impacts our organizations.

---

10. *Id.*
11. *Id.*
12. Raj Chetty et al., Race and Economic Opportunity in the United States: An Intergenerational Perspective (2018), http://www.equality-of-opportunity.org/assets/documents/race_paper.pdf.
13. *Id.*
14. *Id.* at 42.

We Can Remove Self-Imposed Barriers Impeding the Progress of D&I

Institutional barriers require the willingness of policy makers to act, but we do not have to wait on anyone to tear down obstacles within our organizations. Two examples are the law school admissions process and the law firm approach to recruiting law students. It is not necessary to be beholden to 20th-century processes in the 21st century. Research by Professor Aaron Taylor of Saint Louis University School of Law details how the overreliance on the Law School Admissions Test (LSAT) limits entry into the legal profession. Taylor recommends an alternative approach to the LSAT that makes it an additional factor among others that considers what individual applicants overcame to succeed academically based on their unique circumstances. The status quo is not working, so why not try something different? The American Bar Association, legal scholars, law schools, law firms, and corporate legal departments could work together to find ways to remove the current use of the LSAT as a self-imposed barrier. Research in this area suggests progress can occur; we just need the will power to reject an approach we have all inherited from those who came before us.

The law firm recruiting process represents another self-imposed obstacle to diversity in the legal profession. Each year, law firms gear up for on-campus recruiting season by targeting a core group of law schools, hoping to produce a more diverse group of summer associates than the previous class. The general approach is virtually identical in every cycle and the composition of the class is too. Law firms dedicate a substantial amount of resources to recruiting law students and pay them large sums of money without clarity regarding whether or not these students will make effective lawyers. Research by Professor William Henderson of Indiana University School of Law and Professors Marjorie Shultz and Sheldon Zedeck of the University of California, Berkeley, grounded in industrial and organizational psychology identifies how the use of job-relevant factors increases the odds of identifying people who will succeed as lawyers while improving the representation of underrepresented groups in a race- and gender-neutral approach. There are things you can do if you are frustrated by the results generated by your recruiting practices. But are you willing to make structural changes that require you to break from tradition?

A Consequence of Bias Is Unintentional Discrimination, Which Is Just as Harmful

Unconscious bias is a new way to describe an old problem of exclusion that limits opportunities, possibilities, and creativity, and ultimately hurts an organization's likelihood of success. In the 1960s, the country addressed the pernicious consequences of racial discrimination head-on by creating laws to specially address racism. The Civil Rights Act of 1964, the Voting Rights Act of 1965, the Fair Housing Act of 1968, and the passage of affirmative action executive orders by Presidents Johnson and Nixon sought to remedy the legacy of racism and racist policies. Today, in the zeal to create a color-blind society—which should not be the goal because we should never strive to ignore differences—we have refused to openly discuss race. However, being aware of unconscious bias, the existence of which is grounded in extensive social psychology research, allows us to elevate conversations of the harmful effects of discrimination beyond anecdotes.

Bias results in disparate pedestrian fatalities along racial lines, it impacts financial markets, it impacts sports, and research shows how it negatively impacts the critical phases in a law firm attorney's career. Progress comes by, first, acknowledging the existence of bias and that it results in unintentional discrimination that hurts individuals and organizations. Second, in addition to raising awareness, deliberate measures are necessary to root it out. This occurs by, for example, creating objectivity in evaluation and promotion processes, or by pairing junior lawyers with influential senior partners who serve as sponsors—people with gravitas to facilitate access to opportunities positioning them for long-term success. Third, we must accept that the pursuit of bias-free organizations where D&I flourish is a continuous process that will ebb and flow. And, finally, we are not powerless in this pursuit.

The legal profession should represent and resemble the diversity of our nation. We have made progress thanks to the unimaginable sacrifices of previous generations, but much work remains. The baton for change gets passed from one generation to the next, and now it is our turn to continue the work that has benefitted many of us. Let's fix this together. Thank you.

Sincerely,
Kenneth O.C. Imo

Index

H

S

T

Z